The Storm

& the

Tall-Ship Pier

The Narrative Poetry of

David Lewis Paget

1

To my Internet friends,
wherever you are…

Narrative Poetry by the same author:

Timepieces – Poems Out of Time & Other Places
At Journey's End – Narrative Poems Vol. II
The Demon Horse on the Carousel – and Other Gothic Delights
Poems of Myth & Scare
The Devil on the Tree – and Other Poems of Dysfunction
Tales from the Magi
Taking Root
The Season of the Witch
Smugglers Pie
My China
The Red Knight

ISBN – 978-0-9807148-3-8

BARR BOOKS

Poetry Contents

Foreword

Variety, they say, is the spice of life. There is certainly a lot of variety in the narratives that make up this eighth volume of Gothic Verse. The human condition reveals itself in a variety of idiosyncratic ways, and just as the politics of right and left devolve into idiocy and anarchy, so do these stories deal with the extremes of the human condition.

The characters that fill these pages are far from what could be considered normal in a well regulated society. They exist on the fringes of sanity and nightmare, their lives slipping away into mythical regions where, for the most part, there is no possibility of return. As a reader, you too may slip into that abyss of the mind we call imagination, and once fired up you may be carried away into a land where nothing is certain anymore, where the consequences of a step aside from the well worn path may be to open up whole new realms of apprehension or reverie. All that is required of you is the suspension of disbelief, a darkened room, an empty hearth, a creaking door, and an unnatural silence broken only by the wind in the eaves. Then prepare yourself for the first visitor of the night, the figurehead who intones, 'You'll wish you'd never been born!'

David Lewis Paget   March 2014

The Storm & the Tall-Ship Pier

They call it the Tall-Ship Pier, because
It hasn't been used since then,
Its timbers rotted and barnacled,
And black since I don't know when.
The storms it's weathered have taken some,
You can't reach it from the beach,
A hundred yards of its length have gone
The rest is stark at the breach.

But nobody goes there anymore
There's not much left of the town,
Just a couple of old stone walls
The rest is tumbling down,
It sits forever beyond the Point
Where the sailing ships came in,
A crumbling wreck of years gone by
With a hint of forgotten sin.

The winter storms were a testing time,
The seas flooded over the pier,
The ships sat out in the bay, in line
Rode out, this time of the year,
Til when a black-hulled barquentine
Came in with a Dutch command,
The Captain, Herman van der Brouw
In charge of the 'Amsterdam'.

They tied her up to the bollards, just
As a storm was coming in,
A woman stood on the quarter-deck
And the lines in her face were grim:
'You said we'd head to Jakarta,
Not to this god-forsaken place!'
'I told you, stay in your cabin,'
Was the reply, with little grace.

The Captain turned to the bosun,
'Make her secure, but down below,
She's not to come on the deck again
While still in the port, you know!'
The woman struggled, was taken down
But she flung a curse at his head,
'Your time is limited, van der Brouw,
When Dirk finds out, you're dead!'

The wind blew up and the storm came in
And the sea began to swell,
The sky was black and the 'Amsterdam'
Would grind as it rose and fell,
It tore the bollard away from the pier
At the stern end of the barque,
Then slowly swung from the prow out wide
Side-on to the waves, an arc.

It kept on swinging around until
It crashed right into the pier,
Taking a section out with all
The cabins, back at the rear,
The wind was howling around the bow
As the barque sank low at the stern,
A voice screamed, 'Get me the hell from here,
Or van der Brouw, you'll burn!'

The crew were swept off the quarter deck
Were drowned right there to a man,
While van der Brouw had leapt to the pier,
The part that continued to stand,
The woman rose to the surface for
One moment more in the storm,
And screamed from the top of a breaking wave,
'You'll wish you'd never been born!'

They found him lashed to the planking
After a day or so of dread,
His eyes were staring, his face was white
He was just as surely dead,
But something curious came to pass
As they took his corpse ashore
The flesh on his hands was burned and black
With his fingers shaped like a claw.

And she, her body was swept on out
For she's not been found 'til now,
And all that's left of the sailing ship
Is the figure, set on the prow,
A woman, carved as a figurehead
That creaks and groans in a storm,
And seems to mutter against the pier,
'You'll wish you'd never been born!'

The Invaders

'Cata, pick up the children, then
We'll all away to the woods,
They say there's a mighty army come
To steal our homes and goods,
They're capturing slaves along the way
So we need to be aware,
These men of steel with their breastplates on
Take children with fair hair.'

Sca had looked at his wife, she had
The hair of ripened corn,
And so had both of their children from
The day that they were born,
But he was dark, from the Iceni
And his face was painted blue,
He'd come from the beach they'd landed on
Where the blood was mixed with dew.

'I've never seen quite so many ships
They're standing off in the bay,
And way on out, the horizon seems
To be filled with ships today,
They're crushing all that's before them,
Our chiefs are down on their knees,
They know we can't over-awe them
With our spears and charioteers.'

'This army's bringing its mighty gods
And they have this one called Mars,
He rules, they say, each clashing of arms
From way up there in the stars,
Their shields are linked in a solid wall
That we can't get through to fight,
They'll rule us now as they rule the Gaul
So we must be gone tonight.'

They made their way to a hermit's cave
And they found some shelter there,
But the Legion came and they took his wife
For the sake of her golden hair,
His children too, were taken away
From the land of their loving home,
And the people gasped in the marketplace
When the two were sold, in Rome.

While he fled back to the Iceni
And he waged guerrilla war,
Served in the army of Boadicea
Once she had come to the fore.
She stood, six foot and her tumbling hair
Was red, right down to her waist,
'A terrible sight,' the Romans said
As she laid their cities waste.

They'd stolen all of her lands and laid
The lash across her back,
They'd raped both of her daughters,
They were fond of doing that,
They didn't know that the Iceni
As a tribe were more than bold,
Or of the terrible price they'd pay
When they cast her out in the cold.

She wiped out Camulodunum,
And slaughtered the Romans there,
Went on to sack Londinium,
This woman with flame red hair,
She burnt the city down to the ground
While the population fled,
The only people that stayed in town
Were lying in heaps, the dead!

They slew the Hispana Legion
That had marched down from the north,
Went on to Verulamium
And carried a flaming torch,
The Romans there were slaughtered,
The city razed to the ground,
But not before the warrior Sca
Had saved the wife he found.

She'd been enslaved in a Roman house
Had disappeared for years,
And when he pulled her out of the flames
She couldn't see him for tears,
So they fled to the northern borders where
The Romans held no sway,
And their blond haired, blue-eyed offspring,
They still live there today.

The Creek

There wasn't a lot of love to lose
Between Joe Brown and Brent,
Their farms lay either side of a creek
That now lay dry, and spent,
They used to talk in the early days
When they had no axe to grind,
But Brent came back with a bride one day
Who had been on Joe Brown's mind.

But Joe was slow in the love-me stakes
While Brent was a bit more flash,
He'd cut on in at the Farmer's Ball
To the girl with the bright blue sash,
While Joe walked off to sit on his own
And wait for a second chance,
But Brent hung on and dazzled the girl
Right though to the final dance.

The courtship took a matter of weeks
Then they came new-wed to the farm,
And Joe was down inspecting the creek
As Brent showed Jill round the barn,
There wasn't a fence between the two
They used the creek as a line,
'The land to the west is yours,' said Joe,
'The land to the east is mine.'

The balance wasn't so equal now
With a new bride over the way,
Joe would have married the girl himself
But hadn't been game to say.
He soon withdrew to his farmhouse, sat
And wallowed in his despair,
He'd been so set on marrying Jill
There was nobody else out there.

The Autumn rains came on with a flood
And the creek had begun to flow,
Brent stayed at home with his new found love
Not even a thought of Joe,
While Joe lay plotting to get him back
He'd teach him to be so flash,
And walked on up to the top of the creek
With a shovel and old pick-axe.

He felled a tree, and shovelled some stone
To block off the old creek line,
Watched the water form in a lake
Then rested, taking his time.
He chopped a hole in the old creek bank
The water washed it away,
And formed a new creek bed to the west,
And wondered what Brent would say.

When Jill got up at two in the morn
The tide was flooding on through,
In through the back door of their house
And cutting the house in two,
Brent went roaring up to the hill
Astride of his old half-track,
'Have you gone crazy, Joe,' he cried,
'You'd better be putting it back!'

'Too late, too late,' said his surly mate
'The creek is forming a bed,
And anything to the east of it
Is mine, the agreement said!
So move your things to the west of the place
For the east of the creek is mine,
The creek that's flowing right through the house
Will be the dividing line.'

Brent went muttering back to the house
And divided the house in two,
He shored up all the rooms to the west
As the water came tumbling through,
While Joe sealed off the east of the hall
Made sure that his rooms were dry,
While Jill looked over the barricade
At Joe, and started to cry.

'Why have you done this thing to us,
What did we even do?'
'He cut me off at the Farmers Ball
In the course of a dance with you.
You never gave me another chance,
I was waiting to propose.'
'But I would never have married you,
Brent was the man I chose!'

Brent went over and burnt the house
On the other side of the creek,
There wasn't water to fight the flames
So it smouldered there for a week,
The farms are empty and vacant now
Two creek beds, dry as a bone,
With Brent and Jill now living in Nhill
And Joe in the scrub, alone!

I Only Have Eyes for You!

The store had been closed for a month or more,
The Receivers opened the door,
To auction off all the fittings there,
Whatever stood on the floor,
There were counters, mirrors, plenty of stock,
The tills and the rubbish bins,
It was all going under the hammer,
Even a line of mannequins.

When John McRogers happened to pass
He heard the clamour inside,
He peered on in through the window glass
And he watched the human tide,
The bids were coming from everywhere
From phones, and spread through the store,
So he wandered into the human mass
And made his way from the door.

He wandered along the vacant aisles
Saw everything piled in heaps,
There wasn't much of a bidding war
So everything went quite cheap,
He wondered if he should make a bid
Was there anything there for him?
His eyes then came to rest on a girl,
A fabulous mannequin.

She stood in a line of eight or nine
But caught his eye from the start,
He thought that she had the bluest eyes
Of all, and she stood apart!
She must have been all of six foot six
With a tapering line to the waist,
And breasts of promise and silken legs
A woman of style and taste.

He put in a nervous bid when she
Was auctioned along the line,
But nobody put in a counter bid,
And he thought to himself, 'She's mine!'
He had a courier pick her up
And take her straight to his home,
Then stood her up in his office, where
He could savour her there, alone.

She hadn't a scrap of clothing on
They'd taken it off when she went,
He tried to avert his eyes, she showed
No sign of embarrassment,
Her hands hung limply down at her side
No effort to cover up,
But her eyes had followed him round the room,
Whenever he'd start, or stop.

'I'm going to call you Jennifer,'
He said to himself, out loud,
Then sensed she shuddered and straightened up
In a movement that seemed quite proud,
His wife had left him the year before
For a keeper, down at the zoo,
So now he said, and in fact he swore,
'I only have eyes for you!'

'I only have eyes for you, my dear,
My Jennifer from Le Trée,
I'll always cherish you near me here
When I work out here, all day,
We'll spend our evenings here in the warm
With a single desk-top light,
And in the gloom of this little room
You might even come to life!'

He left her naked, stood by his desk,
She had an erotic air,
The wig she wore flowed over her back
Brunette, but the lights were fair,
He worked each night at his desk in gloom
Lit only by one small stand,
And every now and again he'd rouse,
Reach over and touch her hand.

The hand was cold, plastic and hard
And it couldn't return a thing,
Until one night, he opened a box
And slipped on a wedding ring,
He worked away for an hour or so
Til he'd filled out a batch of forms,
Then reached unconsciously out for her hand
To find it was soft and warm.

He looked up into her shining face
And noticed, to his surprise,
Her cheeks had softened, her lips were red
And a lovelight shone from her eyes,
He stood and reached for her willing form
And she did what he wanted to,
But an urgent message tugged at his brain,
'I only have eyes for you!'

'I only have eyes for you,' she thought
And beamed that into his head,
He never would leave that office again,
His friends soon thought he was dead.
They came in force, broke into his house
And found that he'd really gone,
'There's only a couple of mannequins here,
But one of them looks like John!'

The Dream Fish

They say that I came up screaming when
I surfaced, near the boat,
Distraught, they said, eyes gleaming
Thrashing around, could barely float,
They pulled me in with a boat hook, thought
I might be down with the bends,
Then decompressed in a chamber, that
Was where this story ends.

The start was out on a dive boat near
The Isle of Tora Lee,
One of a cluster of smaller isles
Down in the southern sea,
It lay out wide on the outer edge
Of the continental shelf,
'It's one of the greatest dives,' they said,
'But check it out for yourself.'

21

It fell away on the eastern side
A thousand fathoms or more,
Nobody knew how deep it was -
And who was keeping score?
The first three did their shallow dives,
No more than 100 feet,
While I stayed back in the boat to wait,
I had to be more discreet.

The record dive was a thousand feet
With our scuba type of gear,
I knew they wouldn't be happy if
I tried the record here,
I cooked a fish on the after deck
While the rest were down below,
And ate it while I was waiting there
For their heads to finally show.

I checked the depth as I went on down
At a slow and measured pace,
I had to adjust to the pressure as
The fish swam past my face,
I checked the gauge, 600 feet
And I kept on going down,
Til I came to the inlet of a cave
That brought me up with a frown.

For jammed in the entrance to the cave
The remains of a sailing ship,
Just the prow and the forward deck
With the mast collapsed on it,
The stern had broken away and gone
To the seabed down below,
But up at the front, the 'Black Revenge'
Was painted along the prow.

I swam on into the cave, and lit
My way in through the dark,
Hoping to hell I wouldn't swim
In the path of a roving shark,
But fifty metres inside the cave
Was a tiny glow of light,
Flickering up above me like
The stars on a pitch black night.

Then suddenly I had surfaced,
There was air inside the cave,
Pulled myself on the ledge and found
I stood by an open grave,
A line of skeletons in a row
That had once been fifteen men,
They must have known they would never roam
Or take to the seas again.

I sensed in the corner of my eye
A movement in the dark,
Then spun around and I saw her there
A woman, standing, stark,
She wore the rag of a printed dress
And she crossed herself, and hissed,
'Would the good Lord please preserve me!
Be you man, or be you fish?'

I must have looked quite a sight to her
In my rubber scuba gear,
I took off my mask to calm her down
As she backed away in fear,
'How long have you lived down in this cave,
And how did you arrive?'
'I eat of the good Lord's fish down here
And they've helped me to survive.'

She said she'd come on the 'Black Revenge'
As the moll of Captain Tull,
He'd kidnapped her from the 'Bell and Bar'
And had locked her in the hull,
She'd sailed the seven seas with him
Til the storm that set her free,
Swept her into this cave with him
In seventeen sixty-three.

'His bones lie there at the head of the line,
I cut his scurvy throat,
Just as he crawled up on the ledge
When he said he couldn't float.
My name is Mary Parkinson
And I've hoped, and dreamed and cried.
To see my own dear home again,
Before my mother died.'

I didn't tell her the year it was
It would be too cruel to say,
Two hundred and fifty years had gone
But to her, a year and a day,
I told her I'd fetch some scuba gear
And I'd be back down, and soon,
And that was the day I lost my way
On that autumn afternoon.

They said I shouldn't have eaten it,
That fish with the broad green stripe,
The fish had made me hallucinate,
I said that it wasn't right!
'I've seen the woman, deep in the cave,'
They patted my hand, and that,
But I'm fretting that Mary Parkinson
Still waits for me to come back.

Moth!

She started wearing the corpse paint when
She'd just turned seventeen,
Renamed herself Pandora, though
Her real name was Jean,
We thought it was just a cult thing when
She dyed her hair pitch black,
Painted her lips and fingertips,
She looked like a shark attack.

With piercings in her eyebrows, tongue
And thumb rings on each hand,
An ankle chain that proclaimed her game,
'I'm anyone's, on demand!'
She'd go to the Metal concerts or
She'd sit and sulk in her room,
And file her eye-teeth down to a point,
And scare herself in the gloom.

She kept a tin trunk under her bed
That she'd picked up second-hand,
But wouldn't let on just what it held,
She said it was contraband,
We thought that she might grow out of it,
Get sick of being a Goth,
But that was before she came on it,
A huge, Death's Head Hawkmoth.

She'd always collected butterflies
A Lepidoptera freak,
They hung in frames with her Gothic games
And she pinned them every week.
She'd bring them fluttering in a jar
And she'd spread their tiny wings,
Lay them down on a plaster board
And stick them there, with pins.

She brought the Hawkmoth home one day
And she let it out in her room,
She said she wouldn't be pinning it,
It danced to an evil tune.
'It foretells war, and famine, death!'
She said as she watched it fly,
She seemed entranced as she watched it dance
For her mouth was open wide.

I didn't see, but I heard her choke
And I found her on the floor,
Trying to retch the hawkmoth up
As she choked and spat, and swore,
'It flew right into my open mouth
And it's gone right down my throat!
I feel it fluttering way down there,
Will it kill me, if I choke?'

'It's probably dead by now,' I said,
'It couldn't survive your bile,
It's just like eating a turkey roast
You'll digest it, in a while.'
'I don't feel well,' said the Goth from hell,
But she took a sip of Coke,
Then hid away for the rest of the day
Wrapped up in her Gothic cloak.

She'd never been very talkative
But she now clammed up for good,
She'd sit in the gloom of her darkened room,
We thought it was just a mood.
But then I opened her bedroom door
To check on our evil Goth,
And out there flew, more than a few
Of the Death's Head strain, Hawkmoth.

Pandora lay way back on the bed
And her mouth was open wide,
All I could hear was fluttering, fluttering
Coming from way inside,
And moths were flying out of her mouth
In a steady stream to the room,
And all the walls and ceiling, covering,
Moths in the afternoon.

A week had passed from the funeral,
The coffin was sealed with glue,
For moths kept fluttering out of her mouth
With nothing that we could do,
I finally opened her old tin chest
And found it was full of moths,
Of every species, fluttering, fluttering
Out of Pandora's Box.

The Primitive Painter

He was leaning against the wall, backed up
And staring through fumes of gin and whiskey,
Glaring at all the toffs, dressed up
And ravelling through his sordid history.

But never a sense of 'us' with him
He was more like a raging arcane animal,
Caught and caged, as they looked right in
To poke and pry at his painted trammel.

Oils and charcoals, water colours,
Pinned like an insect by their gazing,
Pointing fingers would rape his skin
Pick through his pockets, grinning, gaping.

What would they know of his woods and fields,
The towering oak, or the dew at dawning?

Only the light that a lamp post yields
In the mean streets when the world is yawning.

Theirs was a world of tile and brick
Of diesel fumes and the rail line snaking,
His were the hills of hay and rick
The tumbledown cot and the farmer, raking.

'What did you bring me here to spill?'
He said to the shyster gallery owner,
'There's nothing you couldn't print at will
With a Laser print, and a barrel of toner.'

'They're coming in hordes to see your myth,
You're a breath of air in a jaded Autumn,
A genuine Primitive, Jordan Griff,
I lured them in, and your work has caught them.'

But Jordan scowled and he curled his lip
As the crowd milled using an unknown language,
'I'd rather be down at the 'Rope and Skip'
With a pint of ale and a cold meat sandwich!'

'You're really an artist?' said the woman
Who stood at his shoulder, pale and shaking,
'I like the one at the farmer's gate
With the girl, head bowed, as her heart is breaking.'

Griff looked deep in the woman's eyes
For the chord she'd struck was his secret mourning,
'How did you know?' He'd sobered up,
'I was the girl your paint was born in!'

Jordan halted his glass, mid-sip,
He seized her hand as his heart was pacing,
'Years have slipped between cup and lip,
I'd give them all for a second tasting!'

He led her into a lumber room
And she locked the door as they pulled apart,
Then found some cushions and in the gloom
They lay on the floor there, making art.

That's how his Primitives came to start
With a joy not there at his god-rot dawning,
A horse and cart with his palette heart,
And a tousled woman each tumbledown morning!

Theatre of Dreams

Down at the end of Charters Street
In a dim-lit part of town,
There stands the old Alhambra and
They're going to pull it down.
We warned them up at the council, but
They said it's a waste of space,
There's not been a film for twenty years
Since the Carol Ransome case.

Carol was found in a pool of blood
By the curtains, up on the stage,
Somebody took a knife to her
In a crazed, death-dealing rage,
They never discovered just who it was
But the cinema closed right down,
Nobody wanted to go again
In this hick, one hotel town.

That was the end of our childhood fun
Our own theatre of dreams,
No more Saturday Matinées
Or milk shakes or ice creams,
Nothing to do in this one horse town
But to chase the girls in the park,
And get some serious kissing done
When the day was getting dark.

So Al and Joe and Mary Ann
And me, I must admit,
Broke on into the cinema
And found ourselves in the pit,
Right in front of the dusty stage
Where the curtains hung in shreds,
Barely hiding the giant screen
That was covered in old cobwebs.

We'd played in there for an hour or so
Running between the rows,
Making the Hammond Organ screech
Like a fat man touching his toes,
When suddenly there was a swishing sound
And the curtains began to part,
And something flickered up on the screen
As if it was going to start.

We stood stock still and we held our breath
When the speakers grumbled and groaned,
'It looks like we've got an audience!'
A voice on the speakers moaned.
Then faces peered from the ancient screen
From the days of black and white,
But there wasn't a single projection beam
From the room where it used to light.

A shimmering glow from the screen fell on
The first few rows of seats,
And one dimensional girls appeared
With ice creams and with treats,
The figures spilled from the silver screen
And onto the wooden stage,
Dracula, framed in black and white
And Frankenstein in a rage.

We were all of us petrified by blood
And Al was thinking to run,
But 'Don't you move!' said an ugly hood
On the screen, and pointing a gun.
They made us sit in the second row
And paraded their long-gone fame,
Bela Lugosi's fangs and cloak
And the Hunchback of Notre Dame.

Then as they faded a woman walked
From the wings, and out on the stage,
And a man that we knew as Grocer George
Flew suddenly into a rage.
He knifed the woman a dozen times
And he beat her down to the floor,
And over the screams of Mary Ann
We made a break for the door.

The screen went dark and the stage was bare
And the curtains hung like shrouds,
We said that we'd never go back in there
As we lay, looked up at the clouds,
But we each went in to the grocery store
And we whispered, 'Carol's back!'
'We know what you did,' said Mary Ann
And George's eyes went black.

He chased us out of his grocery
And he closed the store for good,
Then policeman Andy found him hanging
Down in the Maple wood.
They'd better not take the Alhambra down
Or the ghosts of the silver screen
Will all get out, and they'll roam about
Without a theatre of dreams!

A Walk in the Park

'Will you not go walking with me, Michelle,
Will you not come out in the park?
There are lights between each tree, Michelle
So you'll not be caught in the dark.
I have looked for you since the Winter Ball
When you turned, and gave me a glance,
And winked an eye with a long-drawn sigh
Could it be, I'm in with a chance?'

Michelle was walking, her shoulders bowed
With her eyes still fixed on the ground,
The weight of the world was on her back
When she looked aside, and frowned,
'I would love to walk in the park with you
But I can't, there isn't a chance,
For eyes are watching my every move
They report each thing to Lance.'

I'd seen this Lance at the Winter Ball,
Lance Gordon George Dupree,
They say that he's an 'Honourable'
From some vaunted family tree,
But his eyes are beady, his mouth is grim
There's a jealous look in his eye,
And he'd pulled Michelle from the ballroom floor
When he'd heard that long-drawn sigh.

'My father promised my hand to him
When I'd barely turned thirteen,
Exchanged for some of his gambling debts
As my sister was, Lurline,
She hanged herself on her wedding night
In her silk, beribboned dress,
She would rather death than shame, she said
And I shall do nothing less!'

The wedding was barely a week away
I heard, from a friend I sought,
I got a job in the stables there
At La Maison de Villacourt,
I saw Michelle through a window where
They'd locked her into a room,
And watched her cry, and dab at her eye
Through a long drawn afternoon.

They posted a sentry at her door
Let nobody in or out,
I tried to attract her attention but
I couldn't afford to shout,
So I pitched a stone at her window pane
And she finally got the hint,
Opened the casement window then
And smiled, with her eyes a-glint.

I helped her down, onto a horse
And we galloped out of the yard,
I knew wherever we went from there
We'd have to be on our guard,
She guided me to a wayside Inn
Where she slid on down to the floor,
Then threw me a kiss as she clambered in
Post-haste to a coach and four!

'I'll never forget you,' called Michelle,
'And what you have done for us!'
Then kissed the man in the coach and four
As I sat in shock, nonplussed.
'I never promised a thing,' her voice
Came drifting back in the dark,
'But one day soon in the afternoon
We'll take that walk in the park!'

The Man Who Died Each Night

He lived in a tiny attic, set
Way up on the second floor,
I'd never have known he lived there, but
He left his shoes by the door,
A note tucked into the left shoe said
'They're yours if I don't return!'
The right said, 'Put on a dead man's shoes,
And know that you're going to burn!'

The boarding house was for down-and-outs
So you know where my life was at,
The final link in an endless chain
Since they threw me out of my flat,
I had no job, I had no friends
My family moved away,
They hadn't left an address for me
So here's where I had to stay.

I heard him shuffling past my door
With a walk like bone on bone,
His eyes were dim and his face was grim
And his skin as grey as stone,
I chanced to be in the hallway once
But he just stared straight ahead,
I said 'Hello,' but he rattled back,
'I've just returned from the dead!'

He'd sit awhile on the balcony,
In the fading rays of the sun,
Trying to tan the greyness out
But the pallor was not undone,
I grabbed a chair and I sat by him
And he finally looked my way,
His eye delved into my very soul,
'What did you want to say?'

'You look like a man of secrets,'
Were the first words that I thought,
'Maybe you have an insight into
Things that I might be taught?'
'There's nothing here in your life, it's clear,
That would help,' he gave a sigh,
'I only know of the deathly fear
That is yours, when once you die.'

'Nobody knows what happens then,'
I said, 'for it's understood,
Once you have left this mortal coil
You're dead, and you're dead for good!'
The old man shivered and shook his head
'I'm the only one who knows,
For I die nightly in my bed
And return when the first cock crows!'

I didn't believe him way back then,
I hardly believe him now,
But I crept into his midnight room
And I put my hand on his brow.
His flesh was icy cold to the touch,
He had no pulse or breath,
His eyes were pointed up in his head
And I knew he was caught in death.

But still he came on shuffling out
In the first grey light of dawn,
After the cock had crowed, he said,
When his body began to warm,
I asked him what he had seen out there
While caught in the clasp of death,
And he spoke of the chambers of despair
When he finally caught his breath.

'The chambers are lit with a flickering light
From a million candle's glow,
A million tubs of candlewax
That light up the rooms below,
And set in deep in the candlewax
Is the shape of a human form,
The head protruding just like a wick
Who wish they'd never been born.'

'The flames are burning the tortured flesh
The heads are trying to scream,
I pass along them on right and left
As if it's a nightmare dream,
But this is the fate of terrorists
And suicide bombers there,
Their one reward for the cause they fought
An eternity of despair.'

I turned away and I felt quite sick
At the things death held in store,
And all the other horrors he'd seen
When he'd nightly passed death's door.
'How long must you go on suffering this,'
I said, as I turned my head,
But the old man sat in his rocking chair
Quite still, and finally dead!

The Tower

The city was laid like a wasteland
Like a rusting, crumbling sore,
Half of the houses were boarded up
Along a neglected shore,
The spirit had long gone out of it
That had made the city great,
Men fifty miles to the south of it
Were determining its fate.

Way up on the Presidential floor
Was a group of greedy men,
The czars of the old industrial core
Who had bled the town back then,
'The real estate's a disaster,' said
A man who had been the Mayor,
'The auto plants are a rusting heap,'
Said the man who held the Chair.

'We've got more pensioners on the funds
Than workers in the plants,
There's crime and violence in every street
And the Unions make demands.
So what's the conclusion, gentlemen,
Do we give this plan its head?'
'Whatever we do, it's much too late,
The city's as good as dead!'

And that's how they came to build 'The Tower'
To illuminate the sky,
'There's plenty of work for everyone
At a hundred storeys high!'
Nobody knew just what it did
Or what they were building for,
They only knew that they had a wage,
Could hold up their heads once more.

A central lift in The Tower went up
And down ten times a day,
Taking tools and materials
To restrict the Tower's sway,
'They say we're going to go High-Tech
And they're closing down the Plants,
The days of auto's have gone for good
But they won't tell us their plans.'

The Tower was built within the year
With a gaping hole up top,
A semi drove through the streets one day
And by The Tower, it stopped.
It carried a massive box-like thing
With a mass of flashing lights,
Was loaded into the lift, and sent
Up on its maiden flight.

They took it up and it crowned The Tower
While the people watched in awe,
There hadn't been people in the streets
Like this since the Second War.
A massive counter was counting down
As the people stood and cheered,
'I hope it's not what I think it is,'
Said a man with a long, white beard.

While down in the Presidential Suite
Just fifty miles away,
A group of men put their sunnies on
And stood by the window bay,
'Well how do you clear a festering slum,'
Said one, as he watched the clock,
While back at The Tower a sign lit up
And the word was 'Ragnarok!'

The Baker of Warley Copse

On a twisting, winding, rutted track
That weaved from under the pines,
A figure came in a burlap sack
Where the crossroad intertwines,
I could only see the bleeding feet
As they peeped from under the sack,
And the hood hid every feature that
Would deem it a Jill or Jack.

There was purpose in that stolid walk,
And determination fixed,
I thought to offer a helping hand
But my feelings there were mixed,
There were leaves and twigs on the figure's back
And a slime that looked like mud,
I thought that it might have been attacked
When I saw that the slime was blood.

Nothing could stop its slow advance
As it plodded into the street,
I reached on out but it just walked by
So I thought I'd be discreet,
The day was settling into dusk
As it reached the village square,
And just as the ancient gas lamps lit
It gave a cry of despair.

The cry was that of a woman lost,
Was more of a hell-fire screech,
It echoed up to the steepletop
And I thought of Caroline Beech,
The girl who'd gone to the woods one day
For a picnic of pies and mince,
The basket lay for a week and a day,
She hasn't been heard of since.

The figure stopped and its arm flew out
To point at the Baker's door,
I saw his face at the window lace
As pale as a painted whore,
The sweat stood out on his beady brow
As he hurried from room to room,
Locking each door and window now,
And shivering there in the gloom.

A crowd was gathering in the square
Surrounding the baker's house,
'You'd better come out and show yourself!'
But he was quiet as a mouse.
The men of the village burst right in
And they thrust him down on his knees,
She put one bloody foot on his head
And he squealed, 'God help me… Please!'

'I only wanted some love,' he said,
'But you just pushed me away,
I'd never have hurt a hair of your head
If you'd loved me once that day.'
And that was enough for the surly crowd
Who called on Oliver Beech,
To bring a rope from the stableyard
For a lesson they had to teach.

Her father fastened the rope around
The cringing baker's neck,
Just as the daughter's burlap sack
Collapsed to a heap on the deck.
There was nothing inside the hood or sack
As it lay there on the street,
Only the footmark stains of blood
From the murdered woman's feet.

They dragged him down to the wood of pines
And he showed them where she lay,
Under a pile of autumn leaves
He'd covered her with that day,
They left him hanging above the spot
As they bore her gently home,
Now there is no baker in Warley Copse
So the villagers bake their own.

Mother of the Bride

I was introduced to her mother
One Whit Sunday, down at the Hall,
They said that this was a ritual
And suffered by one and all,
She wanted to check your hands were clean
That you had no flaw on your skin,
I wanted to marry her daughter
But if I had, I couldn't come in.

They led me in through the servant's door
Down a passageway to the rear,
Marching me past some gloomy rooms
Was an ancient Grenadier,
He didn't reply to a single word
That I said, his face was grim,
Then into a room with a chandelier
That was gloomier than him.

She sat at the end of a table, veiled
And motioned me to a chair,
The dust was thick on the table-top
And I'm sure there was dust on her,
I'd heard she once was a beauty
One of the greatest in the land,
But she sat there bowed like a coffin shroud
As she raised her withered hand.

'Show me your hands and your fingers,' she
Then whispered in gravel tones,
Her voice like the dying embers of
The ashes of human bones,
I raised my sleeves to the elbows and
I held them out to her stare,
'I'm going to marry your daughter,'
I declared, 'so be aware!'

She flinched, as if I had slapped her
Then she said, as hard as nails,
'I'll write the end of the chapter,
I'll not heed your rants and rails.
My daughter won't marry anyone
That I don't approve, you'll see,
You think that you are the only one
Come cap in hand to me?'

'There was a time, I was in my prime
When the world was at my door,
And I could have married anyone
But the love that I had was poor,
A rival had him imprisoned, just
To get him out of the way,
Then said I could buy his freedom if
I'd lie with him for a day.'

'My love was such that I put my trust
That this Earl would keep his word,
So slept with him on a Sunday, then
He put my love to the sword.
He said that I'd have to keep his bed
For I had no place to go,
That I was fit for playing the whore
And he'd let my friends all know.'

'I couldn't cry, I would rather die
But my first thought was revenge,
My heart was broken forevermore
But my love would be avenged.
I ran his lordship an evil bath
With herbs and salts disguised,
Then held him down while it ate his flesh,
And put out both of his eyes.'

I leapt to my feet on hearing that,
And staggered back from my chair,
'So now you know I'm a monster,
If you cross me, just beware!'
'I think you've told me a pack of lies,
But I love your daughter, true!
I'm going to marry her come what may,
I swear, in spite of you!'

She rose and beckoned me follow her
And she led me through the gloom,
Down through a flagstone stairwell and
Into a tiny room,
A man lay there in an iron bath
That was filled to the brim with oil,
And only his face was still intact
Though his eyes had both been spoiled.

'He hasn't an ounce of flesh on him,
The oil just keeps him alive,
He'll never get out of this bath again,'
But he'd heard us both arrive.
'For God's sake, kill me and end it now,'
He groaned from his oily tomb,
'I will when you bring my Martin back,'
She whispered, there in the gloom.

I couldn't get out of there fast enough
But I'd lost my way inside,
I knew I couldn't get married now
I was far too terrified.
She called me back and she raised her veil
And she said, 'He stole my grace!'
I saw to my horror that syphilis
Had eaten part of her face!'

Misbegotten Heart

I wake and prowl the house at night
And wander through the gloom,
The only light that streams are beams
Of silver from the Moon,
While every room is silent
And the passageways are dark,
There's just one sound, the beating of
My misbegotten heart.

But no-one else is stirring
And the atmosphere is thick,
With dreams and ancient memories
From some old sailing ship,
They rise up from the midden of
A thousand journeys sailed,
That came to grief on some dread reef
As each one said, 'You failed!'

And long-lost faces turn away
Before they'll meet my stare,
I try to capture them again
And say, 'I know you're there!'
They shake their heads in silence and
Then drift into the night,
'I know that I was wrong,' I call,
They whisper back: 'You're right!'

So on then through the early hours
My vigil seeks the past,
Re-visiting each love I lost
As if it were the last,
And tears stream like some sad dream
Repeating: 'Well you know,
Just why I turned away from you,
I really had to go.'

The years have mounted up, and now
Lie on me like a tomb,
Reflected in the silence of
This darkened, empty room,
And just as dawn is breaking I
Cry out, 'I cared, you know!'
My voice, it echoes in the gloom,
'Why do you hate me so?'

The Reflection in the Pool

I'd hidden away the mirrors
Packed them up and sent them off,
Taken the shine off the saucepan lids,
Sandpapered the coffee pot,
Everything that reflected I'd
Sand-blast, like the sliding doors,
Even got rid of the polisher
For shining the wooden floors.

It was very like narcolepsy when
She saw her face on a plate,
She'd go in a trance and sit for hours
In a crazy, dreamlike state,
I'd take away the reflection and
She'd sit and weep for hours,
'You've taken away my beauty,' she
Would say, and take cold showers.

It seemed like a terrible sickness that
She loved her looks so much,
She'd say, 'If you won't let me see myself,
I'll just make do with touch,'
She'd run her fingers over her face
Explore each crease and mound,
And sigh to her satisfaction as
She felt her lips turn down.

I couldn't get rid of the garden pool
That flowed on in from the brook,
Babbling over the standing stones
From the woods at Nether Hook,
I'd catch her kneeling beside the pool
And staring into its depths,
Smiling at each reflection that
Would ripple with every breath.

'Beware of the evil Water Sprite,'
I told her more than once,
'He takes advantage of lovely girls
For he hates to be outdone.
He'll lure you into a shady pool
With guile, and his tender lies
And hold you down 'til you surely drown,
You'll avoid him, if you're wise.'

She told me then of a vision that
She'd seen, that of a prince,
He'd smiled at her from the water but
She hadn't seen him since.
'That's not a prince but the Water Sprite
And he's trying to lure you down,
To put your face to the water, but
I've told you once, you'll drown.'

The water was babbling gently on
A sunny day in Spring,
In shades of the weeping myrtles and
The sound of cuckooing,
Miranda was knelt beside the pool
And I saw her head go down,
When claws reached out of the water
Pulled her in, without a sound.

I raced across and I seized her hair
And I pulled her from the pool,
But claws had raked at her pretty face,
She said, 'I feel a fool!
I should have listened to you, I know
But I thought that just one kiss…'
But he had turned to a monster and
Had bitten her rose red lips.

I put the mirrors all back in place
And I bought new shiny pans,
Polished the floor, you can see your face
But she hides behind her hands,
She never looks in a mirror now
Though her scars are healed and white,
But goes each day to poison the pool
To kill off the Water Sprite.

Puppet Master

There's always been something controlling me,
I knew, but I knew not what,
Something diverting and foiling me
Since the days that I lay in my cot,
I thought it was simply a parent thing
As they whispered their rules in my ear,
The things that were right and the things that were wrong
And the things I would most have to fear.

They sent me to school and the teachers, too,
Must have read from the very same book,
They always laid blame and they said it the same
And the cane lent a sting to their hook.
'You're coming to learn, not to think for yourself,
You'll repeat everything that I say,
And maybe just some of these rules will stick
If you dwell on the rules every day!'

Then once in the world my employers unfurled
All the rules and the regs I would keep,
I didn't last long, I'd seen them before
And told them they put me to sleep.
The government fined and unlicensed me
From a book that they said was the law,
The magistrates sat on a heap of these books
As I shrugged and I said, 'What for?'

I sat in the jail for contempt of court,
Spent plenty of time in my cell,
The world was consumed with a million rules
Designed to consign you to hell.
I watched all the lawyers and prisoners, cops
As they danced to the rules of the cot,
And sensed they were puppets, and most of them fools
Who would baulk at the words, 'I will not!'

They'd hate to be questioned, they thought they were right
And if you disagreed you were canned,
They'd lock you away for a hospital stay
There was no going back, it was planned.
You had to be made to agree with their way
So they clamped electrodes on your head,
Then slide up the volts, and it wasn't their fault
If it happened you ended up dead.

They called it Electro-therapy
And said it was doing you good,
But the thoughts in my brain they were never the same
When I came out from under that hood,
I saw the strings jerking from shoulders and heads
In a vision you couldn't conceive,
And there were the hands that were pulling their strings
When I called out, 'I don't believe!'

'I've never believed and I'll never believe,'
I called, and they all moved away,
A thunderous cracking of mortar and ceiling,
It all fell apart on that day.
The strings fell away from my shoulders and hands
And I knew I was finally free,
And then I called up to the Puppet Master,
'You won't be controlling me!'

People were falling all over the place
As he dropped all the strings from his hands,
The bearded Master could see the disaster,
'You've ruined my world and my plans!'
He paused for a moment and then he was gone
Leaving people to blink in the light,
The rules were the rules of the Puppet Master
Now we can decide what is right!

The Intruder

The wind blew out and the sea rolled in
By the cliffs and the curving beach,
A lonely stretch, they were kith and kin
And had never heard human speech,
A cottage grew by the shore one day
There were figures of surly men,
The sea had muttered, 'They're in my bay,'
And the wind replied, 'Amen!'

The men had left but the cottage stayed
Like a wound to the ocean's pride,
It split the wind at the valley floor
As it passed there, either side,
The sea said 'blow it away my friend,
For it grieves my heart to see,
The works of man where I lap the sand,'
And the wind said, 'Leave it to me!'

It soughed and soared at the eventime
And it scored with sand from the beach,
It struggled to topple the chimney pots
As it surged at one and each,
It lost its puff as the sun came up
When the tide was on the ebb,
'I couldn't move it a jot,' it sighed,
'And the roof, it felt like lead.'

'We'll wait for the winter tides,' my friend,
'I'll surge and wash it away,
I'll undermine its foundations, then
I'll sweep it out in the bay.'
But then a flickering candle lit
From a window, facing the shore,
'There's something a-move, for a shadow flit
Last night through the cottage door!'

The sea had grumbled, 'We'll wait and see
What lingers there in the light,'
The wind peered in at the window pane
And sighed at the wondrous sight,
'A creature there with its golden hair
And its eyes, a deep sea blue,
That set me quivering in their stare,
So what will they do to you?'

The morning saw at the cottage door
A woman all dressed in white,
She wandered along the empty shore
And the sea had gulped, 'You're right!'
He lapped his waters around her feet
As she waded in for a swim,
And said to the wind, 'She's warm and sweet,
And it's sad, but you can't come in!'

Back on the beach, a gentle breeze
Had whispered the woman dry,
Then flitted, scurrying out to sea,
'You've changed your tune, but why?'
'I think we needed that cottage there,
In reflection, let it stand.'
The wind just capered along the shore
As the door of the cottage slammed.

Last Words

The ice drew lace on the window panes
We couldn't see out for a week,
The air had frozen and blocked the drains
And my tears were ice on my cheek.
'Come back to bed and forget her now
She's been gone since the crescent Moon,
Her passing has freed you from your vow
Yet your grief's pervading the room.'

'I need to know what was in her mind
On the day that she passed away,
She left no message of any kind
Why she swallowed the draught that day.
But you were there when she combed her hair,
You were there for the last words said,
She must have told of her deep despair
Or she wouldn't have ended dead.'

'You knew my sister had many moods,
You knew, before you were wed,
She'd lie, consulting the ancient runes
While hiding deep in her bed.
Her superstitions were known, it seems
Her hold on the world was loose,
She drifted half in and out of dreams
But death was what she would choose.'

I shook my head and I walked away,
And ploughed through the drifted snow,
Crunched a trail through the empty streets
To the cemetery gates at Stowe,
The clouds were grey in the sky above
And the snow built up in the trees,
While headstones peered from their icy tombs
Like sinners, down on their knees.

I scraped the ice from the headstone face
That said 'Elizabeth Jane,'
'An Angel fallen to earth,' it said
'While her heart was wracked with pain.'
A shadow fell on the marble face
As I turned, but no-one was there,
Then words appeared like an act of grace,
'My sister killed me - Beware!'

The horror showed on my face, I rose
To follow the tracks I'd made,
But somebody else had left their prints
Leading away from the grave,
The tracks were made at a frantic pace
And they forged on way ahead,
Leading me through the cemetery gates
But Elizabeth Jane was dead!

A storm blew up on the way back home
And had turned the house to ice,
I forced my way up the frozen stairs
To confront Margot Desize.
But she lay frozen with eyes a-stare
And a glance said she was dead,
The horror fixed in her final glare
As a shadow stood by the bed!

A Christmas Gift

'What will you buy when Christmas comes
To show me your love, dear heart?
Will you fill my bower with fruit and flowers
To enjoy while we're apart?
Will you buy the things that you promised me,
Like a bangle for my wrist,
Or a diamond, topaz, sapphire ring,
Or a giant amethyst?'

He stood, head down and he held her hand
As she lay so pale in the bed,
He didn't tell her his job was lost
Or what his employer said.
There were charges he would have to face
That would fill her heart with gloom,
That by Christmas Day he would be away
And not be returning soon.

'I'd rather give you the crescent Moon
As a coronet, dear Tess,
And pluck the stars from the Milky Way
As sequins for your dress,
Then call on the Charioteer, my dear
For your transport to the heights,
Where the gods will fall on their knees to bless
This glimpse of paradise.'

She smiled, then faded away to sleep
And dream of a ghostly tower,
Where her prince stood long at the battlements
At the height of a fateful hour,
An army lay in the fields about
In a siege for her, no less,
'We've come for the Queen of Golders Green,
And we won't leave without Tess!'

While he sat bowed in a lonely cell
And wept at his sense of loss,
He'd only needed another month
And the price would be worth the cost,
He'd not be there when she needed him
As she glided out through the door,
The Judge fixed him with a puzzled eye,
'Just who was the coffin for?'

On Christmas Eve she awoke before
Her heart pit-pattered and stopped,
Her fading eyes had looked to the door
Along with her hopes, they dropped.
But in her hair was a crescent Moon
And stars were all over her dress,
While a Charioteer came into the room,
'I've a chariot here, for Tess!'

The Telephone Box

The footsteps echoed on cobblestones
When a chime rang ten of the clock,
As a sailor making his way back home
Was walking up from the dock,
It was cold and dark for the lights were out
And the street was wet with the rain,
When he came to an old red telephone box
At the side of a narrow lane.

The clouds were black and they opened up
So he stepped in out of the wet,
Dropped his swag as it turned to hail
And lit up a cigarette,
The box was ancient, was George the Fifth
And hadn't been used for years,
But stood in a lane that time forgot
When the rot set in, and worse.

For most of the houses were boarded up
And the weeds had grown outside,
Some had embarked for a tree-lined park
And some of the others died,
It was lonely there in the dark of night
As the sailor waited, he sang,
But stubbed his cigarette out in fright
When the telephone next to him rang.

He stared at it for a while before
He raised it, stopping the bell,
It had an echoing, ghostly sound
Like you hear in a deep sea shell,
The sound of sobbing came to his ear
And he cried, 'Who's there, what's wrong?'
'Oh God, I've waited forever my dear,
I'm locked in the basement, Tom!'

The sailor said that he wasn't Tom
But she didn't appear to hear,
'He's got an axe, attacking the door,
Be quick or he'll kill me, dear!'
The sailor didn't know what to say
But a chill ran up his spine,
'Tell me, what's your address,' he said
'Before you run out of time!'

'I'm straight across from the telephone box,
You usually meet me here,
He's found us out, and he screams and shouts
That he'll kill you as well, my dear!
He just came home from a spell at sea
And called me a cheating whore,
If you don't come over and rescue me
He'll have smashed his way through the door.'

The sailor wanted to say, 'Enough!
It's nothing to do with me,'
But flew on out of the telephone box,
Leapt over a fallen tree,
He raced right in through the open door
And he called, 'I'm here, just wait!'
Then made his way to the cellar door
But all he could feel was hate.

The door was shattered, he walked right in
It was dark, there wasn't a light,
He felt around for a candle, lit
And stared at the terrible sight.
A man lay dead on the basement floor
Where an axe had taken his life,
And there with her throat like an open sore
Was the body of his dear wife.

He staggered, stopped, and fell to his knees
And sobbed like a man insane,
'Oh God, it's true, I did this to you,
But my mind's been playing games.
I thought if I went away to sea
I'd return to find they were dreams…'
As he sliced a razor across his throat
He thought, 'Life's not what it seems!'

The Toadstool Man

He was known as the local Mycophagist
In the dales, the woods and the hills,
What happened was sad, for he wasn't so bad
Just a tad underdone, Toby Gills,
They say that the cord was around his neck,
He was born with a carroty mop,
And a pale white head, he was almost dead
When the doctor had called out 'Stop!'

They cut the cord and they let him breathe,
The damage was already done,
The blood had been stopped to his carroty top
So they said that he'd always be dumb.
But he found a niche where the fungi creeps
And went out collecting the spore,
In a year or two he knew more than you
And the college Professor next door.

He studied his mushrooms with loving intent,
He knew about hen of the woods,
He knew about bracket and shaggy manes, magic
And paddy straw, they were the goods;
He fostered his lobster and hedgehog and oyster
And coral fungi and stinkhorns,
But didn't discern between fly agarics
And toadstools that grew in the lawn.

He grew his spore in a deep, dark cellar
And sold to the folk who came by,
And never would judge between Widow Weller
And the ordinary witches of Rye,
He'd sell death caps, and pigskin puffballs
Not thinking to question them why,
Or who would be eating his laughing Jim's
And whether they knew they would die.

The air was thick and the air was damp
And he fell in the dark one day,
Scattering toadstools into the air
And their spores had floated away,
He breathed the spores right into his lungs
For he hadn't been wearing a mask,
But sucked them in right over his tongue
And they came to his lungs, at last.

I happened to see him out in the street
He was finding it hard to breathe,
He could only take a couple of steps
Then sit on the kerb, to heave,
I tried to help but he waved me away
And his eyes were yellow and cruel,
Then I saw what he'd thrown up on the kerb
Some yellow and red toadstools.

The man was a walking toadstool spore
They were popping up out of his hair,
Pushing their way though his carroty top
In a bid to get to the air,
And his skin was blotched like a puffball, he
Looked up at me, and he cried,
As a giant toadstool grew from his throat
And he lay on his side, and died.

Crème de la Crème

Of all the loves that I've loved in life
There was one, crème de la crème,
She turned my head and she caused me strife
But I loved her, way back when,
I met the woman by accident
As the ex-wife of a friend,
We'd see each other and look away
In a game we called 'Pretend'.

'Pretend' she didn't attract me then,
'Pretend' I couldn't care less,
And she'd 'Pretend' that I held no sway
When she'd hide her eagerness.
We'd say, 'Now, what a coincidence
That you happen to be here!'
But fate provided the incidents
For the best part of a year.

She ditched the guy she was seeing then
And I started calling round,
Just for a morning coffee break
And we'd stare each other down.
There was love and hate in each debate
We'd agree to disagree,
She'd say, 'I'm glad that I'm not with you,'
And I'd say, 'That goes for me!'

But then, if ever I missed a day
She'd say, 'Where did you go?
I had a ride, but I stayed inside
Then in fact, you didn't show!'
And sometimes, when she was out about
I would knock, and feel aggrieved,
'Why weren't you home at ten o'clock?'
I'd say, and she'd look relieved.

We felt a reverse attraction like
The same magnetic pole,
Pushing each other away today
Tomorrow, joined at the soul.
The tension there was electric once
That everything had been said,
And there on a Monday holiday
We tumbled into bed.

Our love was a roller coaster that
Would speed us up to the stars,
Bathed in a perspiration that
Was cold as the planet Mars,
And nothing was ever long enough
It was more like a disease,
For neither of us were strong enough
So we crawled away on our knees.

If love is a desperation to
Cling on to the one you need,
That was the explanation for
The love that we felt was greed.
I thought that I'd found the only one
That this love would never fail,
It was if I had found a holy one
In a search for the Holy Grail.

But nothing will last forever, for
The planets will move along,
Challenging each endeavour, be it
Love, or the right from wrong,
She slowly began to drift away
In search for a sense of self,
Begged for the space to run her race
And left me, high on the shelf.

I spent her absence, caught in a trance
And staring long at the wall,
I knew my soul was lost in advance
When I got the final call,
She fell enceinte with another's child
Though she wanted to come back home,
But I was too hurt to take her back
So I soldiered on, alone.

Of all the loves that I've loved in life
There was one, crème de la crème,
She turned my head and she caused me strife
But I loved her, way back when,
I haven't seen her for thirty years
But she has a place in my soul,
While I am playing the game 'Pretend'
And the world is growing old.

The Seventh Floor

He worked in a great Department Store
As the window dresser's mate,
Carting mannequins, wigs and clothes
From the back through an iron gate,
The store room piled to the roof with props
And the bolts of coloured drapes,
Was dark and damp, and a single lamp
Traced shadows through coats and capes.

The store stood over a hundred years
Was red brick to the core,
And towered above the other shops
Right up to the seventh floor,
They said there were gargoyles on the eaves
That would spout when the gutters filled,
And a Griffin standing with evil claws
That would leave a brave man chilled.

The buyer sat in a closet room
Where he'd watch the assistants work,
And call them in for the slightest sin
If he caught them trying to shirk,
He would warn them once, would warn them twice
He would warn them three times more,
Then send them packing to personnel
Way up on the seventh floor.

Nobody ever came back from there
Not even to punch their card,
Their coats and hats were collected up
And thrown, tossed out in the yard,
The beggars hovered around out back
When they heard the buyer roar,
'Get your faggoty, skinny ass
On up to the seventh floor!'

Peter Peeps had been sound asleep
In the window well one day,
Trying to quell a head of Moselle
He'd imbibed, with Martha Hay,
A girl that worked on the second floor
With a line of maiden bra's,
He'd had as much of a chance with her
As a flight to the planet Mars!

The buyer came to the window well
And he saw him sound asleep,
Then yelled, 'Get up to the seventh floor,
You're finished, Peter Peeps!'
So Peter sighed, and he took a ride
On the escalator up,
Higher than ever he'd been before,
His heart in a paper cup.

On the seventh floor was an old oak door
In a passageway filled with gloom,
A flickering gaslight either side
As he stepped through, into the room,
A metronome was ticking away
In a long, slow measured swing,
When a man in an old Top Hat approached,
'Are you looking for anything?'

'They sent me here to collect my pay,
Is there anything I should sign?'
'You'll get no pay from the Firm today
But you're here, so now you're mine!'
Peter backed to the old oak door
That had latched as he came in,
There wasn't a handle on that side
And the man was looking grim.

'You'll never get out of here again,
You'll have to work for your tea,
I'll fix you up with a ledger, here
It's eighteen seventy-three,
The seventh floor is a time-warp that
Was set when the store was built,
And all of you shirkers end up here
While you're working off your guilt.'

He showed him the rows and rows of desks
Like a mid-Victorian link,
With everyone filling the ledgers in
With a pen they dipped in ink,
And there was Roger, and there was Ann
And there was Fiona Shaw,
He'd watched them once, all weaving their way
On up to the seventh floor.

The windows looked down onto the street
But it wasn't a street he knew,
There wasn't a horseless carriage there
And the other shops were few,
'What if I smash the window here
And jump on out to be free?'
'Then you will be buried before you're born
In eighteen seventy-three!'

Peter Peeps looks out on a world
That had gone before he knew,
Then turns the page of his ledger back
To eighteen seventy-two,
There are rows and rows of figures there
That were written before his day,
But the one thing that he's smiling for
Is the arrival of Martha Hay!

The Dutchman's Mast

In the aftermath of a terrible storm
That stripped all the trees of leaves,
I ventured out when the sun was warm
To check on the roof and eaves,
We'd taken a battering, windows out
And shutters were shattered and lay
All over the floor, what shocked me more
Was what lay out in the Bay.

Our beautiful bay with its azure depths
Had stretched way out to the sky,
Had linked it to the horizon blue
Like a tint from another dye,
But now the smudge of an island lay
Not fifty yards from the shore,
With the wreck of some ancient buildings there
Thrust up from the Devil's maw.

It must have been a volcanic ridge
That had sunk in the distant past,
And lying beside the wreck of a bridge
The remains of a Dutchman's mast,
The ship was wedged by a roofless wall
And was half filled up with silt,
While scattered across the floor of a hall
The glitter of something gilt.

I called Marie, 'You should come and see!'
But I must have seemed distressed,
'You won't believe what the sea's retrieved!'
She called, 'I'm getting dressed!'
I'd pushed the dinghy into the sea
Before she could join me there,
With a flushing cheek that had been asleep
And a comb in her bright red hair.

We rowed on out to the island, we're
The only ones on the coast,
'At least we're getting to see it first,'
Was the one thing I could boast,
We pulled the dinghy up on the land
And made the painter fast,
Then walked toward the glittering floor
That lay by the Dutchman's mast.

'I think that they must be guilders,' said
Marie, and her hands had shook,
'The heads are all of William Three,
They were pictured in some book.'
I said, 'Let's go and explore her then,'
And I pointed to the ship,
But she was filling the leather bag
That she carried high on her hip.

'There may be treasure and precious stones
As well as the guilders here,
This is the chance we've waited for,
We're going to be rich, my dear!'
We walked on up where the silt was high
And found ourselves on the deck,
The timbers under us creaked and groaned
As we searched the ancient wreck.

We fell in the Captain's cabin through
The planks of a rotten floor,
And there was a sight to sadden, he
Still sat by the cabin door,
His clothes had rotted around his bones
His head was down on his hands,
A quill was still in his bony claw
But the book had turned to sand.

I saw Marie had a tearful eye
And I said, 'What grieves you girl?
He had his day, and he's well away,
His was a different world.'
But she sank down on her knees by him
And clutched at his tattered sleeve,
'I knew that I'd seen this ship before
But didn't have time to grieve!'

And then she fell in a trance, and knelt
As if to deliver a prayer,
Started to babble in Dutch, I think
As if I wasn't there.
The timbers creaked and a sudden groan
Had filled that cabin space,
The sound had come from the naked bone
That was once the Captain's face.

I turned, and dashed from the cabin
Climbed a stair that led to the deck,
Jumped on over the side, I had
To get away from the wreck,
I thought that Marie was behind me
As the island began to sink,
And jumped on into the dinghy,
Before I had time to think.

The sea rushed over the island as
It sank back down to the deep,
I call Marie in my nightmares on
The few occasions I sleep.
The island, guilders, buildings all
Sank down again at the last,
And the final thing that I saw out there
Was the tip of the Dutchman's mast.

The Ragman's Dray

Nobody knows where the Ragman goes
In the wee, small hours of the morn,
When he's taken the dray with your rags away
Through the pin-point eye of a storm.
He came to stay while you were away
And your sister gave him your dress,
The one with the dreams and the bright sequins
Sewn in to the lace at the breast.

She said that you wouldn't be needing it
Since your dreams have faded to dust,
When all those hundreds of bright sequins
Were dimmed, and turning to rust,
But the Ragman knew that he'd capture you
If he made away with your dreams,
And sits unpicking your party dress
With a razor blade at the seams.

Your sister Grace has a second face
That she turns when she's not near you,
In a zealous, jealous and carping place
That she keeps well hidden from view,
For nobody gives her a second glance
While she schemes and dreams and plots,
To plant your beauty deep in the ground
With a host of forget-me-nots.

Don't peer too long from the balcony,
Don't stand too long at the edge,
She's loosened the rail you lean upon
And thrown the bolt in the hedge,
A sudden rush and a simple push
Will send you a long way down,
While she prepares her look of despair
As they plant you there in the ground.

I'm only a menial footman here
But my love is stamped on my face,
I'm going to track the Ragman down
And bring him back to this place,
I've seen his dray by a cottage door
In the forest of chills and frost,
And seen the women he buys and sells
Who wander the forest, lost.

Your sister sips on a nightly draught
As she sits and watches the Moon,
Plotting to see the end of you,
I know that it's coming soon.
I'll drop a potion into her drink
And tie her up in a sack,
Then throw her up on the Ragman's dray,
She'll never be coming back.

He'll take her deep in the forest there
To the caves of unshriven souls,
Then put her up on the auction block
And sell her to one of the trolls.
The bolt is back in the balcony rail
And the potion's in her drink,
The Ragman's dray is coming today
And your sister's at the brink!

The Day the Cockerel Died

There's a man been hung at the old crossroads
In the village of Little Deeping,
And in his pockets a couple of toads
That were there when they caught him, creeping,
They bound his arms and they hung him high
On the bough of a mystic rowan,
And filled his stuttering mouth with straw
To quell the spell of his going.

The village is set in a mystery
That was old when the world was growing,
Three thousand years of its history
Is lost to the world, unknowing,
The valley's not in the land of them
Who are yet to stumble upon it,
For men live now as they once lived then
With their wives in a primrose bonnet.

And superstition is rife down there
In the village of Little Deeping,
Where women never reveal their hair
With men in the meadow, reaping,
They take their water deep from a well
And light each cottage with lamplight,
Using a primitive type of oil
That seeps from the soil, in moonlight.

Their brides leap over a witches broom
When the harvest grain is swelling,
Under the beams of a crescent moon
With a bonfire near their dwelling,
They change their partners every year
If their bellies haven't swollen,
Or hang their charms up over the door
So their offspring won't be stolen.

They live their lives by the Druid gods
Who would bring about the seasons,
And never question the rights and wrongs
For nature has its reasons,
Their days began at the break of dawn
To the sound of the cockerel crowing,
An ancient bird with its comb and spurs
That would bring the sun up, showing.

But Tam Eilann was a surly man
Who would often lie in, sleeping,
Dreaming away the early day
While the rest were out there, reaping,
He hated hearing the cockerel crow
As it bid the sun, its rising,
When he said, 'that cockerel has to go,'
He was more than just surmising.

One autumn night, he snuffed his light
Went out in the darkness, creeping,
And caught the only cockerel left
In the village of Little Deeping,
His knife flashed once in the cold moonlight
And left the cockerel dying,
His neighbours hurried to see the sight
Of their only cockerel, lying.

'You've shamed the gods and must pay the odds,'
They said as they bound him, crying,
Then hung him high on the rowan tree
And cursed, as they watched him dying.
The cattle low in the byre still
And the bees, they stay in the hive,
For there's not been a single sunrise there
Since the day the cockerel died.

The Falls of Borrowdale

The sky was a smudge-coloured blue up there
When the sailing ship came in,
With full top gallants and spinnaker flared
Full flight from a world of sin,
The mermaid carved on her prow was proud
As she breasted the salt-licked spray,
Her hair a-stream, as the waves she ploughed
And surged to Ascension Bay.

I'd watched her approach from the Sailor's Rest
That lay way up on the cliff,
'It isn't a question of when,' he'd said,
'Nor even a question of if!
The ghost of 'The Falls of Borrowdale'
Comes in with a clear blue sky,
It happens but once a year,' he'd said
'On the twenty-fifth of July!'

I'd laughed at him in the 'Admiral's Arms'
As he swallowed his seventh ale,
While others listened with frightened eyes
Each face was a shade of pale,
'You'll see it best from the Sailor's Rest,
That ruin, up on the cliff,
But don't get caught by the devil's cohort
Swarming up from the ship.'

They'd scaled the cliff to the Sailor's Rest,
I knew the story of old,
Had slain the crew of the 'Captain Teck',
Or so it was always told,
They'd left the 'Rest' in a sea of flames
For the sake of an ancient feud,
While 'The Falls of Borrowdale' lay wrecked
By the mutineers that crewed.

They'd seized young Molly, the serving girl
Who'd worked at the Sailor's Rest,
Had pulled her hair and had pinned her down,
Exposed the girl at the breast,
They took their pleasure and dragged her out
To the edge of the cliff, and pale,
Then flung her screaming down to the deck
Of 'The Falls of Borrowdale'.

And so it was that I lay with the glass
So firmly fixed to my eye,
Up on the cliff by the Sailor's Rest
On the twenty-fifth of July,
The ghostly ship flew into the shore
Under a mass of sail,
No sign of the crew, no lookout stood
On watch at the forward rail.

The ship ground up on the Daley Rocks
Rose shrieking, up in the air,
Her timbers creaking and groaning with
The mermaid's look of despair,
The crew poured out of the lower decks
And flung themselves overboard,
These phantoms, straight from the devil's lair
To put good men to the sword.

I ran some way from the Sailor's Rest
Lay under a bush, and hid,
I didn't know what to do for the best
But watched, to see what they did,
They swarmed all over the Sailor's Rest
Put everyone to the sword,
Then dragged poor Molly out on the grass
And I cried, 'Please stop them, Lord!'

Then the phantoms stopped as they heard my cry
And they turned, each black as sin,
Molly let out a quivering sigh
And they burst in flames, within,
She stood alone at the edge of the cliff
And she waved, no longer pale,
While the mermaid smiled on the prow of the ship,
'The Falls of Borrowdale.'

The Death Watch List

The spirit of Christmas was here again
As they rocked on up to my door,
The aunts and uncles and cousins, all
I'd not even seen before,
They'd smelt the turkey, they'd seen the tree
With its lights, red yellow and green,
They'd even come with their knives and forks
In case that my own weren't clean.

They came in a rush at twelve o'clock,
'Now we're not too late, we trust?
We got caught up at Aunt Mary's, then
We missed the eleven-ten bus,
She says she'll not be cooking this year
So we didn't have time to lose,
She'll hurry along with a minute to spare
As soon as she puts on her shoes.'

I said, 'Oh good!' as they filed on in
To wash their hands in the sink,
Then counted heads and I gulped and saw
The turkey begin to shrink,
A single bird for eleven heads
Or twelve if you counted me,
I might just get a wing and a prayer
When feeding this family.

They found the chest with the beer in ice
But there wasn't enough for all,
So they corked and drank the fine Rosé
That I'd had displayed on the wall,
They ground the peanuts into the rug
And they spilled Chablis on the couch,
Then kept on stumbling over my feet
And all I could say was 'Ouch!'

They sat around with an hour to wait
While the turkey started to brown,
And talked of family members that
They thought were coming on down,
But then the topic they all enjoyed
Was raising its ugly head,
'You'd never believe,' said Cousin Steve
But Auntie Caroline's dead!'

'I heard she fell from the Pepper Tree
With the pruning shears in her grasp,
Into a deadly swarm of bees!'
You could hear the others gasp.
'And George, remember George, he was
Your Uncle's cousin's son,
He fell right under a train; they said
He had a blindfold on.'

Then Gustave from the German branch
And Heidi from the Swiss,
Had both expired in some dread fire,
I'd not heard any of this!
'Delaney died in Ottawa
When he fell dead off his horse,
And Orson choked on a bottle of coke
That was really chilli sauce!'

I cleared my throat before I spoke
'I would hate to interrupt,
But listening to your Death Watch List
Has made my mind right up.
I don't know a single one of you,
You've not been here before,
But you'll find who you are related to
If you'd like to try next door.'

How It Will Be...

The beach, it circles round to the Cape
As a frame to a Prussian blue seascape,
While cliffs arch up to a vaulting sky
To claw at the clouds just passing by;
    But nobody heeds them now, nor I.

The sea, it grumbles or lies sublime
Content in its deeps, or marking time,
Then storms its breakers onto the beach
In search of the mountains, out of reach;
    With nothing to learn, and none to teach.

The sky, it hovers and looking down
Hangs over the earth, both green and brown
Where nature, in its fecundity
Runs wild and free from the sky and sea;
    And unattended by God, or me.

While cottages lie like a pile of bones
Or an ancient monster's stepping stones,
And none of them cared where man came from
Nor where he went while the sun still shone;
    Once they were here, but now they're gone!

The Witches Hat

Out in the children's playground
On the wasteland, near the flat,
There once was a shiny roundabout
They called 'The Witches Hat',
It hung from a greasy centre pole
And would spin, just like a top,
For once that we set it spinning
It would take an hour to stop.

They painted the Hat in black shellac
So it gleamed beneath the sun,
But stood like an evil entity, in the dark
When the day was done,
We never ventured abroad by night
For the land, we thought, was cursed,
With the Witches Hat a reminder of
Just what had stood there first.

Once it had been a Magic Wood
With Elves, and Grimms and Ghosts,
Witches covens and Goblins ovens
We heard about the most,
The land was cleared for a new estate
And they called the land a park,
But nights you heard the muffled shuffle
Of dancing, in the dark.

It was then that they set the Witches Hat
Up on a pole to spin,
One of us ran around with it
While others sat on the brim,
We always ran with it clockwise
Then stood back to count the spins,
For Mother Malloy had warned us
Never to turn it widdershins.

She said it would stop the earth, and that
The sun would go back down,
The Prince of Darkness lay in wait
For the Witches Hat, his crown,
We thought that she must be bonkers
And we laughed each time she frowned,
But never would spin the Witches Hat
Not once, the other way round.

But then on an Autumn afternoon
When the nights were coming in,
Mother said, 'Take your brother out,
Go take him out for a spin.'
She wanted to clean the house, she said,
'And you're always in the way!'
So I took young Robin out with me,
He'd just turned four that day.

I put him up on the Witches Hat
And I spun, and spun him round,
But Robin was a querulous child
And he cried, to put him down.
So then in a bloody-minded mood
And after a dozen spins,
I stopped the Hat and I turned it round,
And ran with it, widdershins.

It must have been almost dusk by then
For the sun dropped into the ground,
The Moon came up with a silver beam
And it lit the whole surround,
I ran as fast as I'd ever run
And the Hat spun like a top,
Robin sat on the opposite side
So I'd see him, once I'd stop.

I ran until I was out of breath
Then I stopped to watch it spin,
But no-one was on the Witches Hat
And I felt the fear begin,
I searched and scoured the land around
And I crawled beneath the Hat,
The little fellow had disappeared
So I ran back home to the flat.

I'll always remember that awful day,
The day when the fates were cast,
I'd spun him into the future, or
I'd left him there in the past,
I shouldn't have turned it widdershins
But now can't bring him back,
At night it gleams in a pale moonbeam
That terrible Witches Hat!

The Chinese Lamp

I was travelling through the country
That was once East Turkestan,
Keeping my western mouth shut in
The province, Xinjiang,
I wasn't going to linger there,
I had planned to head due east,
And follow the Western Wall to where
They spoke my Shanghainese.

They spoke a myriad dialects
All over Xinjiang,
There must have been forty languages,
And I didn't know but one,
I had to get by with signing 'til
I wandered in through the trees,
Into a tiny village where
A man spoke Shanghainese.

He stood in front of a tiny shop
That was selling drink and dates,
And something evil that looked like worms
All white, and served on a plate,
He said, 'Ni Hao', and ushered me in
And I took what I could get,
Shut my eyes and shovelled it in,
I can taste the foul stuff yet.

But there in the back of the tiny shop
Were a host of curios,
Most of them antique statuettes
The sort that the tourists chose,
But up on a shelf, I saw a lamp
Covered in grease and dust,
I said, 'How much do you want for it?'
'More than your soul, I trust!'

I said, 'It looks like Aladdin's Lamp,
But that was the Middle East!'
He shook his head and he said to me,
'Aladdin was Chinese!
His palace used to be over there,'
And he pointed out to a mound,
A hill of rubble and pottery shards
That covered a hectare round.

He said he'd fossicked the ancient mound
And found all sorts of things,
Cups and plates and statuettes
And even golden rings,
But the thing he found that intrigued him most
Was the finding of that lamp,
He'd dug it out of a cellar there
That was cold, and dark, and damp.

And there by the lamp was an ancient scroll
With instructions in Chinese,
'Don't rub the lamp for a trivial thought
For the Djinn will not be pleased,
There are seven and seventy wishes here
Then the Djinn's released from the spell,
But if you should wish the seventy-eighth
Then you'll find yourself in hell!'

'So how many wishes have now been wished,'
But the old man shook his head,
'If I knew that, would I still be here,
I would rather this, than dead.'
He said that he'd been afraid to wish
For the lamp was ancient then,
Had passed through many since it was new,
Back in Aladdin's den.

I offered to give him a thousand yuan,
But he shook his head, and sighed,
'I'd rather keep it a curio,
It's just a question of pride.'
I raised my bid, ten thousand yuan
And his face broke into a smile,
'For that I would sell my mother's hand,
And she's been gone for a while.'

I paid the money and took the lamp
Then wandered into the street,
Held my breath and I thought of death,
And then of my aching feet,
Shanghai was a couple of months away
If I walked as the rivers flowed,
So I rubbed the lamp and I made a wish,
Woke up on the Nanjing Road.

It only had taken a minute or so
To travel a thousand miles,
I put the lamp in my haversack
And warmed to the Shanghai smiles,
I had a meal, and rented a room
And fell in bliss on the bed,
What I could do with another wish
Was the thought that entered my head.

I'm writing this by the flickering light
Of a candle, stuck in the lamp,
All I can smell is candlewax
And the air in here is damp,
I rubbed the lamp and I made a wish
But smoke poured out of the spout,
The Djinn took off with a howl of glee,
There's no way of getting out!

Coma!

I'd only woken an hour before
And it seemed to cause a stir,
With people pouring into the room,
Coming from everywhere,
They looked excited, stared at me
And I stared right back, confused,
But nobody said a word to me
And I started feeling used.

'What the hell…' I began to say,
But a nurse told me to hush,
Stuck a thermometer into my mouth
Then tried to feed me mush,
She cleared the room and a doctor came
And read my chart with a frown,
'Welcome back to the world,' he said,
'It's changed, since you were around.'

I couldn't make head or tail of this,
I didn't know where I was,
Loaded with tubes, I raised my arms
And flapped like an albatross,
'Let me get out of here,' I said,
'I need to get up and walk!'
'Your legs won't carry you anywhere
Just yet, but we have to talk.'

He said I'd been out a long, long time,
It would take more time to adjust,
To start, he asked if I knew my name
So I told him, Benjamin Rust.
And then I remembered the bicycle
That I'd ridden down to the shop,
And the four wheel drive that had sped right by,
Too bad that it didn't stop!

Then slowly figures came back to me,
A head full of raven hair,
Those pouting lips that had tempted me
And a dimple or two to spare,
She'd arched her brows in a quizzical way
When I'd shown her the double bed,
Then laughed, 'You're getting ahead of yourself,
I first need a ring,' she said.

We'd courted all through the summer months
And made love late in the fall,
I'd said, 'I don't want a part of you,
I'd be content with it all!'
We wed in a little country church
Where the rain dripped down from the eaves,
And strolled from the vestry, hand in hand
As a breeze had fluttered the leaves.

My heart had leapt in that sterile room
As I caught the scent of her hair,
I said, 'Is Jocelyn waiting here?'
The doctor continued to stare.
'You have to know that your world has changed
And the change may bring you tears,
You haven't been out for a week or so,
But over a number of years.'

I was feeling the panic rise in me
As those dreaded words sank in,
'Over a number of years,' he'd said,
As if I'd committed a sin!
And then, 'How old do you think you are?'
I replied, 'I'm twenty-two!'
He shook his head at the foot of the bed,
'There's a shock still coming to you.'

He wouldn't say, and he went away
As I lay there, feeling grim,
So I asked the nurse, 'How old am I?'
But she said, 'Just wait for him.'
At three in the afternoon I sensed
A shadow, stood at the door,
And there was a matronly woman there
Who must have been fifty-four.

She said, 'I can't believe you're awake,
We'd long given up on you,
They asked me to come to the hospital,
And I needed to see, it's true.'
Her hair was grey, but she had a way
That dredged a dream from the past,
She said, 'Do you know me, Jocelyn?
It's good to see you at last.'

The horror rose in my throat at that,
My heart hung still in my chest,
'My God, you look like your mother now…'
'I knew that you'd be distressed.
I got a divorce when you didn't wake
After ten long years in this bed,
I feel so sad, but I wed again…'
Her words, like knives in my head.

I'd lain in a coma, thirty years
Why didn't they let me die?
Jocelyn said she paid for me
In hopes, she didn't say why.
This world is a terrifying place
When you lose the love of your life,
And wake to the loss of thirty years…
I'll slit my veins with a knife!

Saving Grace

I got the call at eleven o'clock,
'They want you to dig a grave!'
It wasn't such a terrible shock,
The message came by a knave.
A serving man from the House of Gull,
That mansion up on the hill,
Where Baron Downz kept his hunting hounds
And the beautiful Grace de Ville.

They often sent me a midnight call
To dig them a grave or two,
Whenever there was a duel fought,
For graves, well, that's what I do!
I dig them deep in the dead of night
At the edge of the Forest Clare,
They pay me a hundred and fifty crowns
You wouldn't know they were there.

For only I know the resting place
Of the Lords that fell by his sword,
Of every man that has tried his will
Each one that questioned his word.
The Baron's known for his bloody mind
And revenge is his only skill,
He gets them drunk on his German wine
And then moves in for the kill.

He murdered the father of Grace de Ville
Then kept her there as his prize,
The night that he tried to have his will
She almost scratched out his eyes,
He keeps her bound by a silver chain
With a lock that tethers her wrist,
And swears she'll only be free again
When her maidenhead is his.

The servants told me he paced the hall
With his patience growing thin,
He'd rage and roar when she locked the door
To prevent him getting in,
There was tumult up in the hall that night
So I knew that there may be blood,
I took my shovel and lantern out
And began to dig by the wood.

At three o'clock in the morning they
Arrived in the horse-drawn hearse,
Slid a coffin out of the back
And laid it down on the turf.
The Baron Downz rode his horse around
And peered in the empty grave,
'A fitting place for the maidenhead
Milady's so keen to save!'

I felt the chill running up my spine,
It raised the hairs on my neck,
Surely he couldn't be so unkind,
But the coffin lay on the deck,
The Baron motioned them all away
And they left with the coal black hearse,
He watched me lower the coffin in
Then turned away with a curse.

'Be sure to cover that coffin well,'
He snarled as he turned to go,
Tossed me a hundred and fifty crowns
Then ambled off, real slow.
I heard a thump in the coffin then
And my heart jumped into my throat,
A muffled whimper, down in the ground
And a scream on a rising note.

I knew my life would hang by a thread
If the Baron came back around,
But still I thought, I'd rather be dead
Than bury de Ville in the ground.
I clambered into that terrible grave
And prised off the coffin lid,
She gasped, and thanked the lord she was saved,
But then came a note of dread.

'You play me false, you'll pay with your life,'
The Baron stood looking down,
And then he began to unsheathe his sword,
The shovel was still in the ground,
I turned the shovel blade side up
And thrust it under his chin
We clambered out of that open grave
And swiftly tumbled him in.

I work for the Lady Grace de Ville
In her livery, red and gold,
I've not been asked for a single grave,
Nor ever will be, I'm told,
I take her out in the coach and four
To ride by the Forest Clare,
And run right over the Baron's grave
Whenever we're passing there.

The Pier of Dreams

Elijah worked at the further end
Of the Port McDonald pier,
His job was simply to keep the light
Bright burning through the year,
All he'd see were the seagulls who
Would swoop and dive in the spray,
As the sea beat up on the jetty piles
On a cold, dark winter's day.

His mother had died of a broken heart
Long after his father fled,
Had loosed the chains of his fatherhood
For a life on the sea instead,
They'd put him into an orphanage
Where he learned to abide the rod,
And found that his supplications and
His prayers fell short of God.

The universe was an empty space,
A vast, unseeing sky,
There wasn't a presence watching him
As they'd said, in the days gone by,
He ached for a revelation that
Would show he was not alone,
A single soul in the firmament
In front of an empty throne.

He'd never managed to make a friend
In the long, sad years of life,
And women, though they avoided him
He longed for a sweet young wife,
His isolation was made complete
When he walked back to his room,
After a night on the lonely pier
In the early morning gloom.

One night a waif from the city streets
Sought shelter from the storm,
Huddled against the cabin wall
Where he sat, both safe and warm,
He heard her shuffle and took her in
And gave her tea from the urn,
And fell in love with her sad, grey eyes,
A waif from the city, spurned.

She came again, and again each night,
They talked until the dawn,
And weaved their dreams and their fantasies
Of a world they'd neither known,
But then one night the Inspector came,
A grim, ungiving man,
Who frowned, and he told the girl to leave,
He said that she was banned.

She waited, shivering in the cold
In the lee of the old sea wall,
Til he came hurrying from his shift
As the dawn spread over all,
He wrapped her up in his coat, and cried
He could do no more than this,
But she clung on to his lonely form
And she gave him his first kiss.

He took her back to his room to stay
And he watched her as she slept,
If she had opened her eyes that day
She would see Elijah wept,
'I won't go back to those lonely nights,'
Was the thought that gripped his mind,
To lose his midnight companion now
He thought, was most unkind.

That night, he told her to meet him there
At the far end of the pier,
'Just as the clock strikes one!' She said,
'I'll be there, never fear.'
He'd soaked the pier in kerosene
Just twenty yards from the end,
And when she arrived, he said, 'You'll see,
They won't part us, my friend.'

At two in the morning, up it went
In a blaze of fire and smoke,
The centre part of the pier ablaze
As they watched it, neither spoke,
A gap appeared as it all fell in
Was extinguished by the sea,
But the end stood tall like a sailing ship
That had set the couple free.

The storm that ravaged the coast that night
Kept the lifeboat on the shore,
They wanted to go and rescue him,
The Inspector said, 'What for?'
While they looked out at the raging sea
Made plans for the world they'd won,
And when the light of the dawn approached
The end of the pier had gone.

The Winter of Her Heart

She was always essentially evil with
Her long, straight raven hair,
Her eyes as black as a midden, and
Her cheeks, so smooth and fair,
Her lips were ripe with the juice of love
Though she had no love to give,
But coloured them with a hint of blood
From her last aperitif.

She lived in an ice-bound castle, pitched
Next to a frozen lake,
Under a towering mountainside
As white as her wedding cake,
The clouds that hung on the mountain top
Were dark and as foul as sin,
And every day was a shade of grey
Where the sun could never get in.

She wandered the dark and gloomy halls
In a fur, but shivered her bones,
Her footsteps echoing off the walls
Her shadow cast on the stones,
The braziers on the passage wall
Would light her way to a room,
The room where a magic mirror hung
Reflected her in the gloom.

The hearth held a blazing yew tree log
That never seemed to go out,
Apart from a sneaking graveyard dog
There was nobody else about,
She'd stand in front of the mirror there
And look at her hard, cold face,
Say, 'Mirror, when will you let me be,
I need to get out of this place!'

The face in the mirror grimly smiled
With a look of evil intent,
'Why don't you visit the dungeons, dear,
You know you need to repent.'
She tossed her head at the steely gaze
As her conscience peered on back,
'I only did what I had to do
To replenish the blood I lack.'

The woman back in the mirror snarled
And she grew long pointed fangs,
Her brow had darkened, her eyes were fierce
'We reflect our rights and wrongs.
The darkness deep in your cold, cold heart
Has entrapped this place in ice,
Compared to what lies ahead of you,
This place is Paradise.'

The woman turned and began to sob
And she paced the flagstoned floor,
There wasn't a hint of the word 'Repent'
As she opened the passage door,
She ran down several flights of steps
To the dungeon underneath,
Then stood and glared through the rusted bars
At her husband, Gordon Reith.

But Gordon sat on the ice cold floor
His back to an icy wall,
The frost had set on his face and hands
He wasn't moving at all,
The puncture marks on his neck were red
With the last of his lifeblood flows,
She'd screamed the moment she'd found him dead
And ripped and torn at her clothes.

And that was the day the blizzard came
To freeze the lake in the night,
Covered the castle and mountain top
In an endless coat of white,
The mirror showed her an evil face
In place of the one she had,
'You'll not be drinking his blood again,
The blood of a corpse is bad!'

She opened the lock of the dungeon door
And she walked right into the cage,
Shook his body and gouged his face
In a wild, impotent rage,
The door had creaked as she turned her back
And it slammed and locked for good,
As the mirror fell from the wall above
And shattered where she'd stood.

A castle sits in a valley green
And beside a wide blue lake,
With mountains towering up above
To a sky where the sun's awake,
You wouldn't know that there once was snow
And I don't know if you should,
But down in the dungeon lies a man
And the woman who drank his blood.

The Seeds of Disaster

The Starship Galaxy III came in
To land in a farmer's field,
There wasn't much of a barley crop
For the seed had failed to yield,
The city lay just a mile away
In a glow of flashing lights,
'I wonder how they manage to sleep,'
Said the Captain, Arzen Kytes.

They'd travelled across the universe
In a push through hyper space,
For seven years at the speed of light
In a bid to seek and trace,
They'd followed the trail of radio waves
From near to a distant sun,
And ended up in the Milky Way
Where the sounds were coming from.

'There has to be life out there,' they'd said,
'We're surely not alone,
We'll send a mission to check them out,
To see what they're like at home,
They must have a crude technology
To be able to transmit,'
And now in sight of the city lights
They were on the verge of it.

'There's oxygen in the air out there,
It's much the same as home,
It's safe to send out a party in
The seven seater drone,
So under the Captain, Arzen Kytes
They flew to a city square,
But the skyscrapers were neglected
And the weeds were thick out there.

They roamed through many department stores
Now empty of displays,
And passed by stores that were boarded up,
'This town's seen better days!'
Nobody walked the city streets
And the Captain shook his head,
'Whatever happened to bring them down,
It looks like they're all dead!'

But then in an old computer shop
They saw a sign of life,
A dozen or so of bobbing heads,
An old man and his wife,
But nobody said a single word
Or looked when they came in,
But kept on pushing the buttons of
Some tool that glowed within.

The old man opened his mouth and spoke,
'You're not from round these parts.
I saw the flivver you just flew in,
We're back to the horse and cart.
This generation is not so bright,
They don't know how to speak,
The gift of language has passed them by
Now all that they do is tweet.'

'When most of the population died
With famine, came disease,
The crops were genetically modified
And killed off all the bees,
So nothing is pollinated now
But the bit we do by hand,
It wasn't enough to save the world
From the greed that ruined the land.'

'But what about all the city lights,
They're flashing still, in truth!'
'Everything came with flashing lights
To hypnotise our youth.
We may get help from a distant star
If they see them flash in space,
But once the power goes off, we'll see
The end of the human race.'

The Captain of the Galaxy III
Flew back to board his ship,
When questioned by the rest of the crew
He frowned, and bit his lip,
'There's signs of a civilisation here
But they've let it go to seed,'
And smiled at the gentle irony,
'The fools gave in to greed!'

The Final Message

He put a flint to the lantern once
They'd walked across the crest,
Were lost in a group of headstones that
Lay hidden from the rest,
And down in a slight depression he
Lit up a certain tomb,
Where the name of Elspeth Trelawney
Was reflected in the gloom.

Trelawney held up the lantern high
While Corby held the spade,
And Gordon Bracks with an old pick-axe
Stood back, he was afraid.
'I fear the spirits are out tonight
In this graveyard of the damned!'
'Get on, and turn up the sod,' he said,
Trelawney forced his hand.

The Squire was quiet and ashen-faced
As the two had bent their backs,
Corby tipping the earth aside
Then standing aside for Bracks,
'The earth is solid, it's packed right down,
We need to pick it loose,'
'Just do whatever you have to do,
There's little time to lose!'

The Squire had buried his Elspeth back
In eighteen twenty-four,
For seven years he had held his grief
But he couldn't take much more,
'I have to see her again,' he said,
To kiss her pale, dead lips,
To stroke the hair on my darling's head
And caress her fingertips.'

She'd taken the coach and four one day
Way out in the countryside,
The coachman, used to a horse and dray,
Had begun to speed the ride,
He whipped the horses and lost the reins
As the coach began to slide,
Tipped the coach in the watercourse
Where Elspeth drowned and died.

He hadn't looked at his lover's face
Before she was interred,
But tried to avoid the loss of grace
In her face that was inferred.
'I only want to remember her
As she was in the flush of life,
Not in the throes of death,' he'd said
When talking about his wife.

They'd rushed to hurry the burial,
On the day that she was found,
Popped her into a coffin, then,
Planted her in the ground,
Trelawney later had agonised
That he hadn't let her lie,
'I couldn't bear her to be around,'
He said, with a tearful eye.

But now he wanted to see her face,
They lifted the coffin lid,
While Gordon Bracks had turned his back
To see what Trelawney did,
The horror showed on the Squire's face
As he gazed into her eyes,
For Elspeth lay in a bleak dismay
As her fate was realized.

Her hands were raised and they looked like claws
They'd scratched at the coffin lid,
The clumps of hair she had torn right out
Was the final thing she did,
And on the lid she had scratched his name
In the torment of the damned,
'Trelawney, may you be cursed by God!'
She'd scratched, with her dying hand.

Two Pigeons

The farm at Little Rottingdeane
Lay fallow for a year,
Since Cromwell's Ironsides had spent
The winter, quartered there,
They'd emptied out the pantry, killed
The cattle, stripped the barn,
And raped the little milking maid
Before they left the farm.

The farmer, Rodger Micklewaite
Lay in his bed all day,
Too sick to raise his farmer's head,
Too ill to bale the hay,
His wife took on the milking of
The milker they had left,
And comforted the milking maid
Who cried, as one bereft.

'The master should be well again,
By early May or June,'
The wife had muttered tearfully
While gazing at the Moon,
But soon a pair of pigeons took
Their places in the loft,
'Lord help us, it's a sign of doom
To curse our little croft.'

The pigeons had been there before
When folk had fallen ill,
And when they came, it fell the same
For death would spread its chill,
And Rodger died, when they appeared
There was no time for grief,
A man called Palm soon bought the farm
To give them some relief.

The milking maid, her belly swelled
Betook her to her bed,
A tiny room that lay in gloom
Beside the milking shed,
She cried and cursed the Ironside
That set her on this course,
'May Satan put a thorn beneath
The saddle of his horse.'

The babe was born by All Saints morn
She'd screamed to see its face,
The head shaped like a helmet or
Some bony carapace,
She only could discern its mouth
With teeth sharp, and ill-formed,
'I cannot nurse this ugly waif,
I've bred the Devil's spawn!'

Then Palm screeched at the sight of it,
Was sick unto his soul,
'I never should have bought this croft
Or housed this Satan's troll!'
The widow made his sickness bed
And counted him as lost,
For pigeons two came into view
And settled in the loft.

Then Palm began to waste away,
She fed him beer and broth,
He died upon the seventh day,
Was buried in the croft,
But then a troop of Ironsides
Rode through there from the moors,
And one of them remained behind
To tend his fevered horse.

'What ails your horse,' the widow said,
The trooper growled with scorn,
'Some fool that saddled up my horse
Slid under it, a thorn.'
The milking maid, recovered then
And thrust into his face,
The baby, wrapped in lace and shawl
To hide its carapace.

'You left a trace of you behind
When last you passed through here,'
The trooper blanched to see its face
Then shook in mortal fear,
The hungry babe went for his throat
And bit with all its might,
As blood streamed from the Ironside
To drown the Devil's mite.

Two pigeons flew into the loft
Just as the trooper fell,
It only took a minute for
His soul to wake in hell,
The widow and the milking maid
Packed up and left that night,
'This time, we're like two pigeons,'
Said the widow, 'taking flight!'

The Other Side of the Coin

The cards had been falling badly for
The man that they knew as Jack,
He'd entered through the scullery door
In a faded, stained old Mac,
He didn't look like he had a buck
Til he reached into his coat,
And pulled a roll of hundreds out
That would choke a Nanny Goat.

They said he could play a hundred down
And a hundred for each raise,
It didn't appear to faze him then,
He said, 'Well, loser pays!'
He fooled them all with his poker face
And he bluffed at first to win,
But by the time that the clock struck eight
His roll was getting thin.

When Diamond Jim played a Royal Flush
And took his final note,
Jack stood up and he shook his head
And reached out for his coat,
'I thought that you'd try to win it back,
You must have more to spare,
I'll wager it all for what you've got
In your pocket, double dare!'

Jack then sat, and his eyes had glowed
As he scowled at Diamond Jim,
Pulled out a tarnished silver coin
And he said, 'Well let's begin!'
They eyed the coin on the table-top
Its head like a man with horns,
'You can't look now at the tails of it
Til you own it, then it's yours.'

'What would you say that coin is worth,
I've never seen its like.'
'There isn't enough in all the earth
To purchase it, by right,
It must be won in a game of chance
As I won it, long ago,
From a man like a Turkish Sultan that
I met in a travelling show.

Diamond Jim dealt a single hand
And he said, 'What if I win?'
'Then you can look at the coin's reverse
And the chaos will begin!'
'I think that you'd better show me now
Before we play this hand,
I'm not so sure that I want this coin
With its evil Goats Head Man.

Jack reached out and he tossed the coin
Which spun for a while up there,
As each man suddenly felt the pain
Of a deep and a dark despair,
It took forever to clatter down
And rest on the table top,
The sign of a Spider facing up,
They thought that their hearts would stop.

For up from the coin the spirits came
Of the ones that they'd loved and lost,
And all of them seemed to be in pain
As the wailing came across,
They lurched away from the table, and
They stood and they shook in fear,
'By God, there's Marilyn Ampersand
Who drowned in June last year.'

The walls of the room then fell away
They stood on a stony beach,
A woman was drowning out in the surf
But totally out of reach,
And Diamond Jim gave an awful cry
From the depths of his shattered soul,
'I'd give the world as a ransom, dear,
To bring you back safe, and whole.'

Then Jack had snatched at the tarnished coin
And flipped it up on its head,
The room returned, they were standing there,
'You can bring her back from the dead!
You only have to possess the coin
Are you willing to play the hand?'
But Jim had wiped at his fevered brow
And shook, he could barely stand.

He took his winnings, all in a roll
And he pushed them back at Jack,
'Just take your coin and your money too
And leave, don't ever come back!
I like my world as it is, my friend,
Though grief lies deep in the groin,
But Marilyn won't be coming back
From the other side of the coin!'

The Tyburn Jig

My brother was twelve years older so
I knew him not so well,
But heard of him in the taverns,
Getting drunk, and raising hell,
My mother said, 'Keep away from him,'
And I did, for many years,
But blood is blood, and a brother should
Help out, though it ends in tears.

He'd done a spot of embezzling,
He'd picked the pockets of Earls,
You never left him to tend a horse
And he wasn't safe with girls,
But he was my brother Toby,
And I was his brother Tim,
I'd often find him beneath my bed
When he said, 'Don't let them in!'

By 'them' he had meant the Runners
Who were active in the Bow,
And some of the old Thief-Takers
With their ruffians in tow,
They roamed the streets with their cudgels
And would lie, just out of sight,
Beyond the doors of the Taverns, when
They turned them adrift at night.

The streets were mean, and were far from clean
Where my brother used to roam,
Despite the pleas of our mother, who
Would beg him to come back home,
But father remained unbending, said
His eldest son was a swine,
'His endless scrapes, a Jackanapes!
He is no son of mine!'

I heard he'd taken a horse and fled
From a stables in the Strand,
'There's little that anyone now can do,
When they catch him, he'll be hanged!'
My mother, crying a flood of tears
As my father cursed and swore,
'I'll call the Runners, or I'll be damned
If you let him through my door!'

So Toby galloped to Hounslow Heath
Along the Great West Road,
Teamed up with the brute Tom Wilmot,
Lay low in his abode,
They'd venture out on a moonlit night
To wait for the latest Stage,
But Tom was never the gentleman,
Or known to contain his rage.

They stopped the coach on a lonely night
'Your money or your life!'
Dragged out a country gentleman,
His maid, and his homely wife,
He wanted the ring on the lady's hand
But her finger held it tight,
So he sawed the finger off as well
With a sharp, serrated knife.

'It was terrible,' Toby told me
As they loaded him onto the cart,
'The screams and the blood, unholy,'
As the horse was about to depart,
They hung him high on the Tyburn Tree
Next to the Wilmot pig,
Not undeserved, but I cried and cursed
As he danced the Tyburn jig.

The Practice Run

The thunder was rumbling overhead
As we walked toward the church,
I whispered, 'What are you doing, girl,
Are you leaving me in the lurch?'
She looked so fine in her wedding dress
But her face was set in a frown,
'You had your chance,' she gave me a glance,
'You're always letting me down.'

I wasn't supposed to be there so
Her father gave me a nudge,
'Sit at the back if you really must!'
He'd always carried a grudge.
'I couldn't sit by to see her tie
Herself to that freak, d'you hear?'
'Just make a sound and I'll knock you down
And throw you out on your ear!'

I looked at the six foot three of him
And knew he meant what he said,
But I couldn't part from Josephine
In truth, I'd rather be dead,
The thunder rumbled and lightning cracked
Exploded the Wishing Tree,
Dropped it across the Vestry path
As if it was meant for me.

The tree had blocked us off from the Church
As the rain came pelting down,
Josephine raised the front of her skirt
And screamed, 'We're going to drown!'
We turned and ran way back to the car
But they locked me out in the rain,
And Josephine turned her eyes away
For my face was racked with pain.

My clothes were sodden, my hair was drenched
As I wondered what to do,
'What can I say to change your mind,
To prove my love for you?'
She wound the window a tiny way,
Said, 'This is a practice run,
The wedding's not until Saturday,
And by God, you'd better come!'

She'd planned it all and had set me up,
Her father sat and grinned,
'I'll be along with a shotgun, so
You'd better be there, my friend!'
I danced out there in my soaking suit
As the rain streamed down my face,
The 'freak' was simply a cousin of hers
I'd thought was taking my place.

She told me we were having a son
Just after I said, 'I do!'
I said, 'Well aren't you the sneaky one,
Why didn't you tell me? True!'
She waited 'til the reception, then
She really took me to task,
I asked her, 'What of the practice run?'
'I thought that you'd never ask!'

139

Last Chance

'The world has left me behind,' he said,
'I live my life in the past,
None of the things that I came to love
Survived, they just couldn't last.
The rails that I rode are overgrown,
The music I loved has gone,
The friends that I made are left in the shade,
Though most of them travelled on.'

The woman who'd answered his ad was sat
Beside him out on the porch,
She'd heard this tale a million times
So she never carried a torch.
She bent her head as she listened to him
And she smiled, her hair was grey,
The years of care were visible there
As her beauty faded away.

'But wasn't it all a wonderful ride,'
She sighed, as she thought of him,
The man who'd always been at her side
'Til he died, his end was grim.
But that was a dozen years ago
And life carried on, though sad,
She wanted to meet a gentle soul
Which was why she'd answered the ad.

'Why would you want to live in the past
When the past is done and gone,
I tip my hat to the past,' she said,
'But the future lures me on.
There's conversation and love to share
As long as there's life and breath,
The future's only a day away,
The end of it all is death.'

He sat up straight and he stared at her
Transfixed by her gentle voice,
The things that stirred in his hardened heart
He'd buried them there by choice.
Behind her eyes was an inner glow
That he hadn't noticed before,
'Could you really bring me to life again?'
He said, and his voice was raw.

'We can take it just one step at a time,'
She said, 'as we did when young,
The world was such a marvellous place
To explore, like a song unsung,
We'll bless the sun coming up each day,
To spread its light through our land…'
Then watched the roll of a single tear
As she reached on out for his hand.

The Prescient Vest

'You've come to the end, it's sad, my friend
But there's nothing more we can do,
Your kidneys have malfunctioned, and
You're at the end of the queue.
You'd best be making your Will out now
Or you may run out of time,
There's just a question of fifteen thou'
You owe for our work, just sign!'

'I'll not be signing my life away
Just now, though it's almost done,
I may be taking a walk someday
But not 'til I've had some fun.
You say I've only a week or two
To spend, and that's at the best,
I'll cram the rest of my living in
With the help of a Prescient Vest.'

The Prescient Vest, the brainchild of
A Silicone Valley clone,
It calculated the path of life
From the life already known,
It fed its images through a brain
That would never live to see
The normal span of the life of man
Through some abnormality.

So Kevin fronted the Institute
And was strapped into a chair,
Fitted with Vest and Headpiece
And was virtually aware,
It drained the memories of his life
That flashed on past his sight,
And stored them into a tiny file
Just less than a Gigabyte.

And then it started to calculate
Beginning with his wife,
It showed her having a sweet affair
With the boarder, Stanley Smythe,
They both attended his funeral
And she leant upon his arm,
And held the wake with a Currant cake
At Stanley's father's farm.

Then Kevin struggled within his bonds
And tried to say, 'Not true!'
But then his favourite daughter came
Quite suddenly into view,
She stole the funeral money he'd
Been keeping in a jar,
Then jumped on into his Thunderbird
And drove off with his car.

She let her idiot boyfriend in
To sit behind the wheel,
But all he could see were dollar signs
And a car he'd like to steal,
He dropped her off at a candy shop
Drove off and left his Pam,
While only a half a mile away
He ended under a tram.

Kevin suffered a minor fit
At the wreck of his pride and joy,
But didn't suffer a single qualm
At the death of the stupid boy,
His job had gone to a minor clerk,
Dumped records in the bin,
The careful working of twenty years
That he'd spent compiling them.

Then Stanley got at his savings and
He frittered them away,
His wife was clueless, she let him sell
The house he'd slaved to pay,
The future, once he had gone was not
The thing he'd visualised,
He strained and screamed at the Techs,
'Just get this thing from off my eyes!'

He staggered home in a mood and took
Some gas from out the car,
Splashed it around the house, and took
The cash from the funeral jar,
He threw a match and it all went up
Though he didn't know or care,
That his wife and Stan were up above
When the flames went up the stair.

He jumped on into the Thunderbird
And went for a long, last ride,
Along the Beachside Boulevard,
And once he had stopped, he died!
They've banned the use of the Prescient Vest
With a raft of bills and laws,
'The future needs to be locked,' they said,
'For the damage it might cause!'

The Village of Helsomewhere

The cottage stood at the outer edge
Of the village of Helsomewhere,
It held a slate on the garden gate
That scribbled a 'Don't Go There!'
It housed a cat and a resident bat
And something that moved within,
A thing unseen that was quite unclean
With various types of sin.

The folk that entered the garden gate
Had never gone back there twice,
When asked, they shuddered enough to state
'It's something that isn't nice!'
The weeds were thick in the garden, and
Had grown right over the path,
And filled with sand by an old wash-stand
The remains of an iron bath.

Nobody walked the bullock track
That led by the old front door,
To go to town, they'd hurry around
A path that was there before,
The cottage stood like an ancient crone
That blighted the village scene,
A pointing finger, pared to the bone
Reminding them what had been.

At night the Moon rose over the ridge
And it cast an evil glow,
Down through the leaves of the eucalypts
To the cottage, far below,
The windows looked like a pair of eyes
As they stared out through the gloom,
While something was rushing around inside
Like a demon in a tomb.

'Perhaps we ought to have burnt it,'
Said the senior councilman,
'It stands alone as our conscience,' said
The crusty old farmer, Stan,
'We have to bleed for our own misdeeds,
Including a lack of care,
Each scream was seen as a nightmare dream
When Lloyd was living there.'

When Lloyd was hosting his dinners for
The girls from a nearby town,
Nobody seemed to question them
For Lloyd was always a clown,
But screams would happen at midnight
And would often be heard at dawn,
When Lloyd was digging his garden patch
By the light of the early morn.

And Lloyd would wave to his neighbours as
They hurried along his way,
Give them a cheery greeting, crack a joke
And say 'Gidday!'
They didn't suspect that evil lay
Inside in that old tin bath,
The one that is filled with sand, and now
Sits there, outside by the path.

One night the villagers crept on out,
And they took it each by turn,
To set a brand to the cottage, then
Stand back to watch it burn,
But something was rushing about inside
In a black and evil cloak,
While screams had seemed to come in a tide
With the dark and acrid smoke.

The embers were floating far and wide
In the haze of a Harvest Moon,
They set up fires in the eucalypts
That rained in the village gloom,
And every cottage went up in smoke
For the villagers' part, they share
In the deaths of thirteen innocent girls
In the Hell of Helsomewhere!

The Dwarf of Nightingale

Nightingale was a hunting lodge
At the time of Baron Blood,
He was holed up there for a month or so
While the Tamar was in flood,
His knights went after a suckling pig
That they brought back to the Hall,
'We'd best be merry and feast, my Lord,
Or there'll be no fun at all.'

The waters rose and it cut them off
By the monastery at Bede,
So they made to raid the Monk's own stocks
And they carried back the mead,
The hounds lay panting around the hearth
And the knights caroused 'til dawn,
But the waters of the Tamar lay
Close round them every morn.

A cottage lay on the old floodway
By the side of a river wharf,
The waters drove a yeoman out
And his wife, a pretty dwarf,
They made their way to the hunting lodge
And begged that they might come in,
'I'm Olaf, you are my liege, my Lord
And my wife is Tamerlin.'

'And what do you bring?' said Baron Blood,
Who looked for a little sport,
'We're all entombed 'til the waters fall,
'So what do you bring to court?'
'I'm simply a yeoman, with one hide
That's drowned in the river mud,
Along with my only ploughshare…'
'That's a pity,' said Baron Blood.

'What of the geld you owe to me,
And how do you think you'll pay?'
'I throw myself on your mercy, Lord,
To pay you another day.
The river flooded the pasture, and
My crop lies under the mud,'
'Perhaps your wife has a way to pay,'
Said the musing Baron Blood.

'You'll wait at table and serve the mead
And carve the suckling pig,
And feed the hounds at the hearth tonight
While your wife can show a leg,
We'll have her dancing from dusk to dawn
Each knight can take his turn,
For Tamerlin pays your geld tonight
If she lasts from dusk 'til dawn.'

Then Olaf looked at his Tamerlin
And he brushed away a tear,
But she looked bold at the Baron Blood,
'I will stand the test, no fear!'
They helped to set up the feast that night
And they whispered soft and low,
'If one should harm a hair of your head
I will kill, before I go!'

She put one finger up to her lips
And she whispered, 'I'll be true!
I'll not be whirled off my feet by one
Who is half the man as you.'
She took a skewer and she stuck the pig
Right through to the other side,
'I may be small but my heart is big
And I'm still your darling bride.'

The sun went down and the mead came out
As he went to feed the hounds,
The Baron called on a lute to play
From a doorway to the grounds,
Then Tamerlin had begun to dance
And sway as she said she would,
Her dress had swished on the earthen floor,
Out where the Baron stood.

The knights were steadily getting drunk
And the Baron stood and swayed,
'Now hitch that dress to your waist,' he said,
'If you want your geld to be paid.'
She dropped her eyes and she blushed, and cried
But she lifted up her dress,
To show the legs that were short, deformed
And the Baron laughed, no less!

The Baron laughed and the knights had laughed
At the legs of Tamerlin,
She dropped the dress and she burst in tears
And she cried, 'You've seen my sin!'
They didn't ask her to dance again
But they drank until the morn,
Then fell about in a drunken swoon
As she lay apart, forlorn.

A silence fell as the sun came up
When she rose and took a skewer,
Walked to the sleeping Baron, and
She thrust it in his ear,
She thrust it in til it came on out
All blood on the other side,
'You won't be laughing again,' she said,
'Or shaming Olaf's bride!'

They took a skewer to every knight
And they did the same to them,
In, and out at the other side,
A Hall of skewered men,
The waters, they were receding as
Her head, in pride upheld,
Remarked, 'It's time we were leaving,
We have truly paid the geld!'

Nightingale was a hunting lodge
That sank in a sea of mud,
You'd have to dig right down to find
The body of Baron Blood,
The woods grew up in the pasture fields
And covered the grisly tale,
Where lovers walk and will cease their talk
At the song of a Nightingale.

House Proud!

I only wanted a quiet life
Was the first thought that I had,
When the woman beat on my cedar door,
I thought that she must be mad.
She beat and beat, and would not retreat
Though I begged her just to go,
But she cried, 'He's going to murder me,
You must let me in, I know!'

I peered out through a crack in the door
Just to see the woman's face,
Her lips were bloody, her eye was black
And the tears had left their trace,
I groaned I wouldn't become involved
But knew in the end I would,
I opened the door and let her in,
Her hands were covered in blood.

'Don't drip that blood on the carpet!'
She just turned to me with a shrug,
'I've taken the carpet cleaner back
I borrowed to clean the rug!'
Too late, too late, as she smeared the blood
All over my pristine wall,
'Are you callous or just plain crazy?
He'll be coming to kill us all!'

'Then why did you come to me,' I cried,
'There's a hundred doors out there,
Go pick on another married fool
With a life lived in despair.
I never fell for the gender trap
For it always ends like this,
A bottle of Jack with a drunken lout
Who had promised married bliss.'

I steered her into the bathroom, ran
The taps as I heard him roar,
'Come out you blanketty wilful witch
Or I'll have to beat down the door!'
My cedar door with the frosted glass
That I only installed in June,
I heard a splinter, and then a crash
As he burst on into the room.

I pointed the shaft of the toilet brush
At him, from under a towel,
'I've got a gun and I'll use it!' But
All that he did was howl.
A bullet whistled on past my head
And shattered the shower screen,
'I swear I'll blow you to Kingdom Come
If you don't come now, Doreen!'

'For God's sake, give it a rest,' she said,
As she washed the blood away,
Wiped her hands on my nice clean towel
As I groaned in my dismay,
He put the gun in his pocket, dropped
His head and began to weep,
'Is this the guy you've been seeing then?'
'What him? The guy is a creep!'

'He's more concerned with his carpet
Than a lady in distress,
I'd rather you with your Looney Toons
Though you tend to make a mess.'
She walked on up and she kissed him
And they walked out hand in hand,
'Who's going to pay for the damage, then?'
I called, but they had gone.

I never answer a beating door
No matter how long they knock,
I call out, 'Sorry, I'm not at home,'
As I click the fifteenth lock,
A beaten wife is a world of strife
For the man who intervenes,
The bodies may pile outside my door
But I keep my carpets clean.

The Man with the Eyes of God

I met him first in a darkened room
Of the Club called Heaven's Lair,
You wouldn't look at him twice, in fact
You'd swear that he wasn't there,
He'd sunk right into a corner lounge
And you'd think it rather odd,
He sat there facing the wall, and stared,
The Man with the Eyes of God.

I'd drank at the bar a dozen times
But I'd never seen him round,
A patron pointed him out to me
His lips not making a sound,
He turned a beer mat over, then
He nudged, and gave me the nod,
Scribbled a note that said, 'That's him!
The Man with the Eyes of God.'

I smirked, and carried my drink across
Though the patron said, 'Beware!'
Approached the back of the lounge to see
When the man just said, 'Stop there!
Don't venture into my vision, or
You will see what you should not,
Your blood will curdle within your veins
And your heart will surely stop.'

I stopped, and sat to the rear of him
Behind, and off to his right,
'They tell me you have a precious gift
To do with the Maker's sight.'
'It's not a gift, it's a curse,' he said
'That I've laboured with for years,
For God sent me for your history,
And lent me his eyes and ears.'

'He wanted to know what you had done
Since he last went past this way,
And scattered the Tower of Babel by
Confusing your tongues that day,
He hadn't wanted to interfere
For he gave you all free will,
So sent me as his emissary
To report both good and ill.'

'And what have you told almighty God,
The truth, or a pack of lies?'
'I haven't needed to tell, he sees
The truth through both of his eyes,
I feel the sense of his discontent
At you breaking all his laws,
Polluting his beautiful planet
With the scourge of your endless wars.'

'So what does he plan to do with us,'
I whispered there in the gloom,
'Does he plan to come and punish us,
Will our God be calling soon?'
'His spirit has always been right here,
It's embedded in the earth,
In every tree and the mighty sea
In rain, and the gift of birth.'

'You'll feel the wrath of his discontent
In a thousand days of drought,
In ice that clings to your window-sills
In floods that you can't keep out,'
He turned his head and he looked at me
And I cringed at his vacant nod,
For blood lay thick on each cheek, where he
Had put out the Eyes of God!

The Pot Belly Stove

The cabin had sat at the edge of the woods
Since Eighteen fifty-two,
It still belonged to our family,
So I guess that meant me too,
I found myself in need of a roof
And they hadn't been there for years,
So I swallowed my pride, and hitched a ride
And forced the door with a curse.

It was down on the Tasman Peninsula
Was built by my fifth great-great,
He'd been picked up in a London mob
And suffered a convict fate,
He'd done his time with the cat 'o nine
And had broken rocks for the road,
For seven years and a bucket of tears
He'd suffered the convict code.

His Ticket-of-Leave had set him free
So he'd headed into the woods,
Taken a common law wife with him
And a few of their paltry goods,
He'd cleared a section and cut the trees
For the cabin that sits in the grove,
And the one embellishment that he brought,
An American Pot Belly Stove.

The stove still sat in the corner there
It hadn't been lit for years,
I sat on the sagging miners couch
Gave way to a fit of tears,
The branches of trees had ventured in
The water was drawn from a well,
The door at the rear just hung and creaked,
I thought I'd arrived in hell.

I lit an age old paraffin lamp
That luckily still had fuel,
Searched my bag for a scrap to eat
But all that I had was gruel,
The sun went down and the dark set in
To the sounds of the wind outside,
Rustling through the tops of trees
And the leaves of the trees inside.

At midnight, I awoke with a start
To the sound of an evil roar,
More like a man than an animal
Standing at my front door,
I braced myself by the door, it roared
And then it began to pound,
'What do you want?' I screamed on out.
'You're sitting on hallowed ground!'

'I want what's properly mine,' it said,
'And then I'll leave you alone.'
My teeth were chattering then, in fright
When it gave out another groan.
'I'll never rest 'til I get it back,
I need it to make me whole,
A hundred years since they carved me up
I've waited to claim my soul!'

I looked across to the ancient stove
Where a mist was rising up,
A pale blue mist from the rusted flue
And I thought, 'That's it! Enough!'
The mist was taking a human shape
The shape of a surly man,
Wearing an age old Warder's cap
But lacking a good right hand.

I crawled across to the iron stove
And I opened wide the door,
The bed was full of the clinker they
Had burned there, years before.
But buried deep in the ashes there
When I brushed aside the sand,
I saw a shape that had made me gape,
The bones of a human hand.

'Is this the hand you are looking for?'
The thing gave out a groan,
'Come out, and push it under the door,'
I heard the creature moan.
I did, then packed my bag and I burned
The cabin, deep in the grove,
I'll never go near a house again
That has a Pot Belly Stove!

Dorazamite

The children wanted a puppy dog
But I always told them no,
We only had an apartment, with
No place for it to grow,
They groaned and wailed 'til the wife had paled,
'You'll have to shut them up!
They're driving me stone crazy,
All they want is a tiny pup.'

'It can't be done, they make a mess
And they're always underfoot,
I'll get them something inanimate
From the net, I'll look it up.'
I finally found a Russian site
Where they sold some crystal seed,
'Try growing your own Dorazamite,
It's the only pet you'll need!'

I sent away for a starter kit
And it took a week to come,
A couple of packets of crystals
So I bought an aquarium,
The screed said 'Just add water, then
Sit back to watch it grow,'
The kids weren't very impressed, they said:
'It seems to grow so slow!'

'It takes a while,' I began to smile,
'But Rome wasn't built in a day!'
'We only wanted a puppy dog
To take outside, and play.'
It had started forming crystals, but
I gradually forgot,
And failed to check the aquarium,
Whether it grew, or not.

One day the kids were excited, said:
'It's starting to move about,
It ate the couple of skinks we found,
And keeps on getting out,
I found it down on the kitchen rug
In its blues and greens and golds,
But cut my hands when I picked it up,
Too sharp for me to hold.

A week went by and I heard them cry
'It's taken a lizard shape,
Has run right under the microwave,
It's trying to escape.'
'It's only a pile of crystals, it
Can't walk, or snap its jaws…'
'It can,' they said, when they went to bed,
'It's become a Dorazasaur!'

That night, the sounds of a tinkling had
Prevented me from sleep,
Like chandeliers in the wind, the sound
Was making my flesh creep,
The door burst open at three o'clock
With a jangling-wrangling roar,
And there was a glittering lizard, standing
There at the shattered door.

With a crystal eye, and four foot high
Its teeth were red, and sharp,
Its claws were very like amethysts
That tore at me in the dark,
It chased me out to the balcony
When I stood aside, it leapt,
Down to the concrete driveway
Where it shattered across the steps.

We live in a dangerous neighbourhood
Where we have to be on guard,
Where crystal birds, and crystal rats
Run out in your own backyard,
There are crystal dogs and crystal cats
That attack, and eat, and fight,
All from that lousy crystal pack
They called Dorazamite!

The Final Escape

'There's something amiss with you today,
There's something that isn't right,
I heard you weep in your fitful sleep
As you tossed and turned all night,
We've been together for forty years
You've never been so distressed,
You've raised my fears with your silent tears
Why are you sad, my Blessed?'

'A vision came to me overnight,
An angel with sparkling wings,
His face was glad, though he made me sad,
He said, 'It's the end of things!
The end of your careworn duties here,
The end of your struggle and strife,
The end of a long and loyal love
As a true and supportive wife.''

'Just what did he mean by that,' I said,
As I felt my face turn white,
I grasped her hand like a drowning man
And I held her close, and tight.
'Perhaps it was just a silly dream
Like the one that you had before,
The one about Michael, tapping, tapping
Tapping at our front door.'

'Maybe it was,' my wife had sighed
As she languished there in my arms,
'But maybe again, he'd not have died
If I'd listened to his alarms.
He'd said that he hated swimming then,
And later I felt a fool,
The man at the door was tapping, tapping
To say he'd drowned in the pool.'

I felt the quiver of sadness then
That rattled through to the bone,
Our son was lost, and we paid the cost
In our small, but loving home.
She hadn't wanted to look at me
For a year, or maybe two,
His picture flat on the mantelpiece
When she said, 'He looked like you!'

I couldn't deal with her sadness, for
My grief was hard to atone,
We walked like ghosts through an empty house
We both felt we were alone.
The years went by and our love revived
In a way that showed we cared,
The grief that came like a nightly thief
Was held, thrust down, and shared.

'Perhaps it's best that we let it go,
I feel so tired and wan,
I can't remember the love we shared
Before our boy was gone.'
'Your love was all that I wanted, Jen,'
My tears began to flow,
'The angel's name, it was Michael,
You'll just have to let me go!'

The Mock Wedding

She lived there still, in the house on the hill
Though she hadn't been seen for years,
The Lady Margaret Hermanville
She'd lived in a mist of tears,
Her wedding day had been bright and gay
When her groom arrived at the door,
The devious Baron Wűrrtenberg
With his soldiers, back from the war.

The wedding service was short and sweet
Was held by a priest defrocked,
Was hurried through from the point of view
Of all that the Baron mocked,
He'd only wanted her dowry then
But claimed he wanted her hand,
And with it the House of Hermanville
With a thousand acres of land.

She'd gone alone to her wedding bed
While the Baron caroused 'til dawn,
And lay awake with a constant ache,
What had she done, so wrong?
He made his quarters down with his men
While she languished up in her room,
But sought an audience then with him
On the following afternoon.

'Where is the love you promised me
When you came and begged for my hand?
I may be wed but I'm now in dread
That you wanted me for my land!
Prove to me you've a noble heart
That there's more to you than a gun,
And take your bride, for my barren womb
Should be stirring now with your son.'

The Baron laughed, and waved her away
'It's enough that you have my ring,
You have the title of Wűrrtenberg,
Of my heart, not even a thing.
I have a frau in Bavaria
Will be coming to live here soon,
So get you away to the Servants Hall,
You and your barren womb.'

The Lady Margaret stood in shock,
A tear had formed at her eye,
Her face as pale as the clouds that formed
Above on an azure sky,
'I'll go and petition the Cardinal,
I'll have this wedding annulled.'
'You'll not be leaving this house again,'
He said, and her eyes had dulled.

A year went by and she sought some peace
Below in the Servants Hall,
While he went riding to fox and hounds
And didn't see her at all,
His Gretchen came, to lord it above
At the feasts for his Men-at-Arms,
A flashy, rude, Bavarian trull
Who was loose with all of her charms.

The Baron watched her flirt with his men,
Grew angrier by the day,
He had her locked in an old sow's pen
And sent all his men away,
He said, 'You want to live like a pig
Then I'll give you your heart's desire,
He fed her truffles and day-old slop
And she slept on hay from the byre.

Back in the hall, he paced and paced
His echoing feet alone,
Began to think about Margaret
And thought that he might atone,
He heard the merriment down below
Drift up from the Servants Hall,
Went down the cavernous limestone steps
Where his wife was sat by the wall.

'What's this?' he said, as he wandered in,
His wife was seven months gone,
The servants gathered around her there
And her face, it fairly shone.
'You'll never guess who the father is,
It could have been one of two,
You sent me off with a barren womb
But the only Barren is you!'

'So pack your bags, you can leave us now,
You should have been more aware,
The deed of settlement that you signed
For my dowry said, 'Beware!'
The house and land wouldn't pass to you
But devolve to my first born son,
It could have been yours, but now, you see
It belongs to my little one.'

My mother never married again,
I'm lord of all I can see,
A thousand acres of farming land
My mother bequeathed to me,
I've watched her cry and I've watched her mourn
That I'm not the son of a Lord,
I'm proudly the son of a working man
With a mother that I adored!

The Barley Stooks

There's a silence out in the fields tonight
Where the barley sheaves are stooked,
Their shadows stand in a menacing line
While the wives at home are spooked,
They peer from windows, they peer from doors
And they lock their shutters tight,
There isn't a man in the valley's span
For they didn't come home tonight.

They left their cottages there at dawn
As the sun was on the rise,
Wandered out with their ploughman's lunch
And rubbed the sleep from their eyes,
They carried their sickles across their backs
Their fagging hooks and their flails,
And who could read took a crumpled book
To read with a half of ale.

They bent their backs to the task ahead
Of reaping the sheaves of grain,
The clouds were billowing overhead
And they said, 'It looks like rain!'
The sun went in and the sun came out
As the shadows flitted across,
They stooked the sheaves at an angle so
The rain would drain from the crops.

The rain held off 'til the afternoon
When the men were streaked with sweat,
They sheltered under the Sycamores,
Laid down their tools in the wet,
The wives were busily cleaning homes,
Preparing the worker's tea,
They didn't look out to the barley field
'Til the sun dipped into the sea.

They didn't look, it was almost dusk
When they noticed something wrong,
The men would usually come back home,
They'd hear them, singing a song,
A silence settled upon the land
And the wives came out to stare,
But nothing moved in the barley field,
The men were just not there.

Their faces white in the pale moonlight
The wives sat still, and stared,
The stooks were seeming to move about
And the women, they were scared,
The stooks lined up in the barley field
Like a pack of hooded ghouls,
And lying right in the midst of them
Was a heap of reaping tools.

There's a silence out in the fields tonight
Where the barley sheaves are stooked,
Their shadows stand in a menacing line
While the wives at home are spooked,
They peer from windows, they peer from doors
And they lock their shutters tight,
There isn't a man in the valley's span
For they didn't come home tonight.

The Age of Steam

The news spread over the countryside
As a clatter from iron rails,
The ominous sound of clacketty-clack
From their intersecting trails,
The plodding Goods of the 0-4-0
To the proud Express from Cheam,
It muttered as it was going past,
'They're going to get rid of Steam!'

The sudden shock brought an answering hoot
From the stack of the proud Express,
That whispered by on its 4-6-2
But shuddered to draw its breath.
'And what will they pull their Pullmans with?'
As it passed through an April shower,
A 4-6-0 on another track:
'They're moving to diesel power!'

The steam from the Earl of Erin laid
A trail through the valley floor,
Its coals glowed red from the firebox grid
As the fireman shovelled more,
A Day Excursion that quietly sat
To wait for the train to pass,
Had whispered, 'Sorry to see you go,
You're King of the Master Class.'

The smoke that billowed from out the stack
Had turned from white to black,
The footplate shuddered, the furnace roared
As it raced along the track,
'They say they're moving to diesel power
And they're getting rid of steam,'
The Earl of Erin had hurtled by
As a Tank Engine had screamed!

The driver, checking the frantic pace
Was trying to slow it down,
But nothing worked, not even the brakes,
'We're headed for Hampton Town!
We shouldn't be doing sixty-five
We're twenty over the top,
He slammed the door of the firebox shut
And the fireman's shovel dropped.

The tender's couplings opened up
And the Pullmans fell away,
The Earl of Erin had surged ahead
With a new found power that day,
It passed a struggling 0-4-0
As it headed toward the sea,
Gave one long blast on its whistle then
To say, 'I'm finally free!'

The fireman jumped at the water tower,
The glass was going down,
The driver jumped when it hurtled through
The Halt at Hampton Town,
The Earl of Erin went racing on
When the sea came into view,
But locked the brakes at the water's edge
Just as the boiler blew.

The Earl of Erin's a rusted wreck
That still sits there on the line,
And children crawl on its footplate there
And dream of another time,
A time of dragons, a time of trains
A time they can only dream,
The age of romance, gone at last,
It died with the age of steam!

The Diagnosis

'Why do you stay by the window, Jill,
Why do you stand and stare?
There's nothing to see but the sentinels,
The names of the dead out there.
There's more to life than the cemetery
That ranges over the hill,
I'll close the shutters and pull the blinds
If the sight disturbs you, Jill!'

She sighed and turned then, back to the room
But she wouldn't meet my eye,
She'd been morose since the last full Moon
But wouldn't be telling me why,
I thought it might be our child that bloomed
And blossomed under her gown,
But every time that I questioned her
She'd put me off with a frown.

She'd been along to the doctor's, and
Since then, she hadn't smiled,
I asked her, 'What has he told you, then,
Is something wrong with the child?'
She shook her head and she told me, 'No!'
But she wouldn't meet my gaze,
She was always a terrible liar,
Women lie in a number of ways.

I caught her scribbling out her Will
On a parchment page, or two,
I said, 'Why now?' And she looked at me,
'I needed something to do!
I thought it time that we wrote them out,
It wouldn't hurt you as well,
We have to think of the baby now
As my belly begins to swell.'

I sat beside her and wrote it out
If only to calm her down,
She seemed so close to the edge of tears
That I wrote of the love we'd found,
And all I had would belong to her
Who'd saved me from the abyss,
She'd turned this drunken head around
And given a life of bliss.

She squeezed my hand as I signed my name
And the tears rolled down her cheeks,
Her hormones must have been pulling her down,
She'd be like this for weeks,
'You'll feel all right when the baby's born,
We'll sit in the sun, outside,
And get some colour into your cheeks,'
But Jill broke down, and cried.

A week went by, I was far from well
So she made me stay in bed,
'I'm going down with a flu of sorts,
I feel so thick in the head.'
She brought me soup and she tended me
Like a mother hen with a chick,
She cried a lot and she lied a lot
While I lay there, feeling sick.

I staggered out of my bed one day
And stood, looked over the hill,
The snow had feathered the headstones white
I shivered there in the chill,
She came, was standing beside me, then
Reached down, and felt for my hand,
'You know I'll love you forever, Ben,
There won't be another man.'

I looked at her in alarm, I thought
She might be going away,
'What did the doctor diagnose
On that distant day, in May?'
'I knew it would have to come to this,
He gave me results, it's true,
Though not of the tests he did on me,
But the ones that he did on you!'

I write this on the side of the bed
For I find it hard to stand,
My heart is feeble, my body weak
With its cargo of contraband,
But still Jill stands by the window there
And she weeps, and bows her head,
I say, 'Why stare at the sentinels,
Engraved with the names of the dead?'

Footsteps!

I set out on a filthy evening
Jogged the stream and under the bridge,
Headed into the pouring rain
And over St. Alban's Ridge,
I heard some footsteps running behind
But never could turn to see,
For who would venture out in the rain
Just to be following me?

I'd heard the following steps before,
Had stopped, and I'd turned around,
Scanned the bushes and hedgerows
There was no-one there to be found,
I thought I could hear some breathing
From a bush, or hid in a tree,
Though nothing stirred but a restless bird,
Nothing that I could see.

I'd always travelled the leaf strewn path
By the early sun of the day,
But sometimes ran when the darkness fell
By the light of a moonlight ray,
I loved the scent of the pine fresh air
It made me alive, and free,
It wasn't until I courted Claire
That the footsteps followed me.

They'd stop whenever I stopped, and then
Would start again when I jogged,
I thought at first it was just a trick,
An echo, bounced off a log,
But sometimes, there in the silence when
I stopped while catching my breath,
I'd feel the hairs beginning to stir
Way up on the back of my neck.

I turned to run by a farmer's field
That was stacked with new mown hay,
Reflecting light from the pale moonlight,
Awaiting the farmer's dray,
I heard the footsteps behind me squelch
In the mud from the driving rain,
I called, 'You'd better come out tonight,
By God, or I'll cause you pain!'

I pulled a glittering knife blade out
I'd hidden, deep in its sheath,
Scanned the track by the farmer's field
And the heather, down on the heath,
But nothing stirred in the pale moonlight
Though I saw its tracks in the mud,
And as I watched in a gathering fright,
They seemed to be filling with blood.

I turned and ran in a panic then
And weaved my way through the trees,
My heart was beating, my mind was numb
I slipped, and fell to my knees,
I finally found the giant oak
Where I knew that a corpse would lie,
The moon was sending a single beam
And lighting the dead man's eye.

I'd propped him there when I'd slashed his throat
To free up the hand of Claire,
She'd been bereft when he disappeared,
Would never have found him there.
I'd meant to come back, bury the bones
But still he sat by the tree,
And now the footsteps joined with him there,
His eye was glaring at me.

They followed a trail of blood, they said,
The searchers said, when they came,
And I was cowering by the corpse,
They said that I was to blame.
They've put me here in a darkened cell
Where I sit and stare at the floor,
And hear the shuffle of footsteps there
On the other side of the door.

The Port of Dreams

I once had a special friend at school,
His name was Daniel Hare,
He would dream through maths and geometry
For his mind was never there,
I would nudge him in the ribs each time
That the teacher turned to look,
And slide my hand across, to turn
To the right page, in his book.

He'd get this distant look in his eyes
And slump back into his seat,
And tell me then at the break, he'd been
In Ireland, digging peat,
He'd roam the great Canadian Plains,
Was there at Austerlitz,
And hid in a London cellar with
His mother during the Blitz.

The only subject he really loved
Was the study of history,
And then he'd sit on the edge of his seat
Enthralled at the mystery,
But Physics, Maths and Biology
He said, was leaving him cold,
He'd rather be there with Francis Drake
On a search for Spanish gold.

We went our separate ways, of course,
I didn't see him for years,
Then came on him in a boarding house
Where he'd suffered some reverse,
His life, he said, was a shambles, he
Could never hold down a job,
His mind had continued to wander
From Berlin, and to Cape Cod.

His eyes were sunken, his skin was grey
I noted his sallow cheeks,
'I dream too much in the day,' he said,
'And I just can't get to sleep.'
I walked with him in a lonely cove
Where the moonlight shed its beams,
'I need to find me a ship,' he said,
'And sail to the Port of Dreams.'

I asked him why he never had met
And married a local girl,
He said he'd met a girl in his dreams
But she didn't live in the world.
'She waits for me on the other side
Of a wide and windswept Bay,
Not in this life of broken dreams,
She leaves at the break of day.

A week went by and a storm came in,
He wasn't there by the stove,
I made my way in the pouring rain
Where his footsteps led, to the cove,
I found him sat, his back to a rock
With a wild, unseeing stare,
And knew he'd gone to follow a dream
As the sea spray soaked him there.

For out in the bay a Barquentine
Had pitched and tossed in the storm,
A ghostly lantern hung from the mast
As the spars and the timbers groaned,
A figure clung to the foredeck yards
And waved as the wind had screamed,
While the barque turned west where the sun had set
And sailed for the Port of Dreams.

The Hermit

I well remember the Hermit who
Lived up in the public park,
He never ventured out of his cave
Til the sky and the fields were dark.
He was, '...the only Neanderthal
That survived the coming of Man!
Don't get too near or you'll rouse his fear
And he'll chop off both your hands!'

The cave was deep and mysterious,
It hadn't been there for long,
The entrance had been uncovered by
The blast of a German bomb,
As kids we'd run in the daylight sun
Right up to the entrance there,
And scream 'Hello!' in a long echo
When the other kids would 'Dare.'

Then deep within came a rumbling
Like an Ogre, clearing its throat,
In seconds then we were tumbling
And I tore my best blue coat.
Just once we saw him out of the cave
With a beard, down to his waist,
Shaking his fist and grumbling
So we screamed, took off in haste.

The years went by and I asked my Dad,
'Just who was that Hermit guy?
The one that you used to scare us with
In the public park, near Rye.'
He pursed his lips and his face was grim
'Aye, that was a tale, my son,
Back in the war, a soldier there
And a bloody great Ack-ack gun!'

The Germans used to come every night
And the guns would open up,
With searchlights all criss-crossing the sky
We'd get no sleep or sup,
The guns would go, 'Ack-ack, Ack-ack,'
Which is how they got their name,
The Home Guard took it in turns to shoot
Each time that the bombers came.'

'Well Martin Shaw was an older man
And he shot a Heinkel down,
He stood and watched as it burst in flames
Then dived, and hit the ground.
But then a Dornier dropped a bomb
And it hit beside the gun,
It blew a hole in a cave below
Surprising everyone.'

'The gun fell into the cave below
And so did Martin Shaw,
We said, 'That's it, poor Martin's gone,
We won't see him no more!'
But he survived in the cave below
And refused to come on out,
So when they were trying to rescue him
They were looking up the spout.'

'The first one trying to come in here
Is going to lose his head!'
Martin screamed at the rescuers,
'Come in, and you'll be dead!'
He fired a couple of Ack-ack shells
To underline his case,
So they all backed off, and went to tea
And left the gun in place.'

'The years went by and he stayed in there
Long after the war was done,
They knew that he didn't have any more
Shells, for the Ack-ack gun,
So he'd only walk abroad at night
Catch rabbits and steal his veg,
They said he suffered from shell-shock
And was pretty near to the edge.'

My father had almost had me there
'Til I saw his sneaky grin,
'You've had me on again,' I said,
'You really suckered me in!'
He laughed, 'I haven't the faintest who
He was, but just a loon,
But there, that's something to tell your kids
On a Sunday afternoon.'

The Voice in the Upstairs Room

The house that I rented was falling down,
I picked up the place for a song,
There weren't many rooms that were liveable,
The plumbing and wiring were wrong,
I lit up a paraffin lantern there
To lighten the dark and the gloom,
But while still exploring, I thought I heard
A voice in the upstairs room.

I hadn't been up in the loft 'til then,
I'd not even mounted the stairs,
The rooms were a midden of broken toys
Of lopsided tables and chairs,
I carted the worst of them out the back,
The fire that I set lit the gloom,
Again from a window above me there
Was the voice in the upstairs room.

I couldn't make out a word that it said
It grumbled and mumbled and moaned,
I stood and I listened and scratched my head
And to tell you the truth, I groaned.
I didn't know what lay above me there
A squatter, a thief or a ghost,
A thief didn't matter, a squatter I'd scatter
What worried me most was a ghost.

I went and I stood by the bottom stair
Looked up, with a feeling of doom,
The voice was whispering somewhere there,
'You'd better be leaving here soon!'
'The only one leaving this place is you,
Whatever, whoever you are!'
'The only way you will be rid of me
Is by putting the lid on the jar.'

I plucked up the courage and took the stairs,
Was running, but two at a time,
The dust was heavy and thick up there,
Whipped up as I started to climb,
A haze was suffused in the room at the back
Where the window was beaming in light,
And there at a ghostly harpsichord
Was sitting a woman in white.

I stood stock still as she started to play
Bach's Little Prelude in C,
The notes hung quivering, shivering in
The haze of the air by me,
I saw right through the woman, the dress
And the harpsichord to the wall,
There was no substance that I could see,
No substance to them at all.

The music stopped, she was looking at me
And she let out a long, loud sigh,
'I've only played for two hundred years
To some visitors, passing by.
It's never the same as it was at court
With the crinolines, bustles and lace,
And most have fled when the music played,
Without ever seeing my face.'

I looked at the jar on the mantelpiece,
A Funeral Urn with its store,
And ash was spilling, leaving a trace
With the lid that lay on the floor,
I bent to touch it and pick it up
But the woman had let out a cry,
'I pray sir, never replace the lid,
For then I would surely die.'

I placed the lid on the Funeral Urn,
Turned back to look at her face,
The room was empty, the harpsichord
Had gone, not leaving a trace.
There was no sign of the woman in white
And the haze had faded away,
I turned and slowly descended the stairs
With a feeling of vague dismay.

For weeks I scrubbed and I tended that house,
Installed all my goods and wares,
But often found I was listening for
The sound of that voice upstairs.
So I crept in there on a winter's eve
And I slipped the lid off the jar,
Went silently down the stairs again
Still listening, from afar.

The harpsichord struck a strident note
And it woke me up in my chair,
Then suddenly she began to sing
In a voice that was sweet and fair.
I only cover the Funeral Urn
If the vicar is passing by,
But sometimes sit at the head of the stairs
Just to hear the woman sigh.

The Woodland Mass

She wore a net that covered her hair,
A shawl in a peasant green,
A ragged dress that covered her breast
But with nothing in-between,
Her legs were scratched and covered in mud
And her feet were shod in clogs,
I wouldn't have noticed her passing, but
For the barking of the dogs.

She looked aside at the dogs that barked
And she made an evil sign,
Sent them panicking back to the barn
And I called, 'Hey you, they're mine!'
She looked at me from under the net
With glittering eyes of scorn,
'Your dogs will not recover themselves
'Til the Black Beast comes, at dawn!'

I stood agape and I watched her pass
To the shade down by the creek,
She kicked her clogs on the dewy grass
And she washed her legs and feet.
I wandered down and I stood aside,
'You're a stranger to these parts!'
'I've been away, but I think I'll stay
'Til the Mass of the Woodland starts.'

It wasn't really a village then,
Was more a scatter of homes,
Built on the edge of the woodland where
The cottagers laid their bones,
The cemetery wandered into the trees
With the headstones, green with moss,
And each was graven beneath the green
With a dark, upended cross.

'The people here are strange, you know,
They don't like passers-by,
You'd best be moving along before
The sun sinks in the sky.'
She laughed a terrible laugh that sent
Cold shivers down my back,
'I'm only here for the sacrifice,
You can tell your Brothers that!'

The people came from the cottages
At dusk in their hoods and capes,
Wandered into the ancient hall
Half hid by its ivy drapes,
They genuflected before the font
With its rust and bloody stains,
That sat before the upended cross
On a wall that was hung with chains.

A man stood tall at the podium
In a hood that hid his face,
I caught a glimpse of the mask he wore,
A skull that he held in place.
'The ravening beast will be abroad
When the Moon is full and round,
We have to be at the woodland creek
Before the beast comes down.'

He led the way to the woodland creek
Where the girl had sat in wait,
'I hope you've chosen your sacrifice
For the time is getting late.'
A cloud then blotted the moonlight out
And we heard a beastly roar,
The girl had gone when the moon had shone
And her clothes lay on the floor.

And in her place, a hideous beast
As black as a lump of pitch,
Leapt on one of the Brothers there
And dragged him into a ditch.
It mauled and ripped at his carcass there,
He didn't have time to scream,
While I took off, back to my croft,
Away from the nightmare scene.

I lay in the barn, beside my dogs,
They seemed to be terrified,
I sat and loaded my .22
My eyes were open wide,
The Beast came prowling around at dawn
Just as the girl had said,
I shot it once, and between the eyes
But the girl lay there, instead.

Grasscutters

I was sent to work at the old Repat.
It was forty years since the war,
Those ancient diggers would sit and swear
At the pain of the limbs they wore,
The wounds would open as years went by,
They'd come for another slice,
That war was never over for them,
And morphine was paradise.

I saw one veteran struggle and curse
As he ripped at the buckles and straps,
The new prosthesis had rubbed him raw
As his knee began to relapse.
He tore the leg from his wounded stump
Sat on his bed, and roared,
Then swung the article over his head
And flung it across the ward.

The others had ducked as the leg took off
And bounced off the opposite wall,
'I'll have to report you,' the nurse exclaimed,
'It's a good leg, after all!'
'You wear it then,' was the man's response,
'For it's driving me insane,
What would you know of Flanders Fields?
You wouldn't deal with the pain!'

My job was to settle and calm him down
So I asked him about his leg,
'When and where did you lose it, Dig?'
The veteran tossed his head.
'You've heard of a place called Flanders Fields
Where the bullets came in like hail?
Well, I was there with the Anzac's, son,
At a place called Passchendaele.'

'Our Generals were trying to murder us,
I swear, on my mother's head,
They kept on sending us over the top
Until half of the men were dead.
The German gunners would enfilade
As we struggled against the mud,
I'll never forget the battlefield,
It was spattered with bones and blood.

They'd send artillery shells across
At the height of a soldier's knee,
We'd watch them come as they parted the grass,
They were Grasscutters, you see!
Well, I was running with bayonet fixed
And praying for God's good grace,
When suddenly I was lying there,
I'd tumbled, flat on my face.'

'It's strange that I never felt a thing,
When the Grasscutter got me,
It took a while 'til I saw my leg
Was gone, from under the knee.
But that was the end of the war for me,
The end of the life I'd known,
I spent some time back in Blighty, then
I came on a ship, back home.'

I never chided those men in there
Though they'd curse and swear, and roar,
For every man was a hero where
They'd trudged in mud through the war.
That Repat. job was a fill-in job
And I left, still young and hale,
But I never forgot the Grasscutter
Or the man from Passchendaele.

www.ingramcontent.com/pod-product-compliance
Lightning Source LLC
La Vergne TN
LVHW051629080426
835511LV00016B/2259